Rel

Regal, Robin
and Kitten

All ohv-engined models from 1962:

Regal (598 cc and 701 cc) 1962 to 1973
Robin (748 cc and 848 cc) from 1973
Kitten (848 cc) from 1975

Owner's Handbook/Servicing Guide

by C D Barge T Eng (CEI), AMIMI, AIRTE

ABCDE 411
FGHIJ
KLMNO
PQRST

£1.75 C HH

Acknowledgements

Special thanks are due to the Reliant Motor Company for their assistance with information and illustrations. Cars were kindly loaned for photography by Tim Snook, Gerald Putt, and Richmond Park Motors Ltd. of Bournemouth.
Valued advice on lubrication was given by Castrol Ltd, and on spark plugs by the Champion Sparking Plug Company. The bodywork repair photographs were kindly supplied by Fibreglass Ltd (Reinforcement Division), St Helens, Lancs.
The workshop tasks were carried out by Brian Horsfall and photographed by Les Brazier, and the layout of the pages was planned by Lee Saunders.

A book in the Haynes Owner's Handbook/Servicing Guide Series

Edited by Robin Wager

© Haynes Publishing Group 1978

Published and printed by the Haynes Publishing Group, Sparkford, Yeovil, Somerset BA22 7JJ

ISBN 0 85696 411 5

Contents

1967 Regal 21-E Saloon

What's in it for You?

Whether you've bought this book yourself, or had it given to you, the idea was probably the same in either case - to help you get the best out of your Reliant Regal, Robin or Kitten, and perhaps to make your motoring a bit less of a drain on your hard-earned cash at the same time.

Garage labour charges can easily be several times your own hourly rate of pay, and usually form the main part of any servicing bill; we'll help you avoid them by carrying out the routine services yourself. Even if you *don't* want to do the regular servicing, and prefer to leave it to your Reliant dealer, there are some things you should check regularly just to make sure that your car's not a danger to you or anyone else on the road; we tell you what they are.

If you're about to start doing your own servicing (whether to cut costs or to be sure that it's done properly) we think you'll find the procedures described give an easy-to-follow introduction to what can be a very satisfying way of spending a few hours of your spare time.

We've included some tips that should save you some money when buying replacement parts and even while you're driving; there's a chapter on cleaning and renovating your car, and another on fitting accessories.

Apart from the things every Reliant owner needs to know to deal with mishaps like a puncture or a blown bulb, we've put together some Troubleshooter Charts to cover the more likely problems that can crop up with even the most carefully maintained car sooner or later.

There's also a set of conversion tables and a comprehensive alphabetical index to help you find your way round the book.

If the bug gets you, and you're keen to tackle some of the more advanced repair jobs on your car, then you'll need our Owner's Workshop Manual for your Reliant model, which gives a step-by-step guide to all the repair and overhaul tasks, with plenty of illustrations to make things even clearer.

5

1973 Regal 3/30 Saloon

6

The Reliant Family

The familiar Reliant three-wheelers have been around for many years and in fact the story of the Reliant company itself goes right back to before the second World War.

The Regal Mk I model was first shown at the Earls Court Motor Show in 1953, fitted with an Austin 7 side-valve engine and a few fibre glass body panels just to keep the weight down. A Mk 2 version followed, and then in 1956 the Mk 3 version was introduced, which had a body made entirely from fibre glass mounted on a strong box-section chassis. This design has made the Reliant one of the longest-lasting small cars around.

The Regal Mk 4 had wind-down windows and a much improved interior, and continued in production until 1961. The Regal Mk 5 was yet again an improvement on the preceding models, having improved rear-seat headroom, and was the last of the Reliant three-wheelers to be powered by the well proven side-valve engine.

The overhead-valve Regals were introduced in 1962 in saloon car and van form, and were designated the 3/25 series. The power unit was the Reliant-designed manufactured all-aluminium 600 cc engine. Subsequent years saw minor changes including the 21E version, with its added instrumentation and lights, in 1967, but it was not until August 1968 that any major change was announced, with the introduction of the 3/30 series with a 700 cc all-aluminium engine for both the car and van.

Production of the Regal range continued until 1973 when the Robin models were introduced. The Robin sported a 748 cc engine and a completely redesigned body, giving the car a nicely 'rounded' appearance. The gearbox fitted to this model now had synchromesh added to first gear as a standard fitting on both the Robin and Super Robin models. In 197 the engine was upgraded and grew to 848 cc.

It was in 1975 that Reliant launched a four-wheel model call the Kitten which was based on he Robin. (It wasn't the first time that Reliant had attempted to break into the small car market with a four-wheeler – back in September 1964 they brought out the Rebel, which was pleasing in appearance but unfortunately didn't seem to catch on). In the case of the Kitten Reliant are more optimistic and remember, a cat has nine lives!

We've grown to think of the Reliant solely as a three-wheeler and as a stop-gap for the motor-cyclist who wants the roominess and comfort of a car without the expense of the increased road tax which one usually associates with a four-wheeler. The Kitten, on the other hand, may appear on the surface to be a Robin with an extra front wheel, but Reliant feel that fuel economy is the principal attribute of this model, along with a body which won't rust.

Here's a summary of the main landmarks in the development of the range, starting with the introduction of Reliant's own engine.

7

1972 5 cwt Supervan 3

1978 Super Robin 850

1977 Special Edition Robin GBS

1978 Kitten Estate

1978 Kitten Saloon

1962   Reliant first fit their own 600 cc all-aluminium engine to the Regal 3/25 Saloon and Mk 4A Van

1963   Regal 3/25 van introduced in place of the Mk 4A version

1965   Regal 3/25 Super Saloon introduced, similar to the 3/25 Saloon but with different radiator grille and separate lens for side lamps and indicators, reshaped rear end of body, and repositioned handbrake lever

1966   The Supervan (based on the Super Saloon) replaces 3/25 model

1967   De Luxe Saloon and Supervan 2 introduced with modified engine and improved interior

1967   Regal 21-E introduced as a luxury version of the De Luxe Saloon. The 21-E represents the 21 extras added to the basic specification!

1968   Introduction of the 3/30 series fitted with a 700 cc all-aluminium engine for both the car and van models

1973   The end of the Regal range – production gives way to the Robin range which utilizes a 748 cc all-aluminium engine in either Basic Saloon, Super Saloon or Super Estate versions

1975   Engine uprated to 848 cc and capable of returning approximately 70 mpg at a steady 40 mph

1975   Kitten range introduced as a four-wheel version of the Robin with a top speed of 80 mph

1976   Super Kitten Estate version introduced

1976   De Luxe versions of the Kitten Saloon and Estate introduced, with better trim, revised switch layout and improved suspension

Road Test Data taken from

The figures published here are extracts from *Autocar* magazine road tests (except Regal model).

Fuel consumption: The mpg figure is the overall consumption figure for their test period, including performance testing. Many owners will achieve significantly better consumption figures. The formula on the right provides a guide ('**mpg**' refers to the quoted overall test figure).

Driving style	Driving conditions		
	severe −10%	average	easy +10%
Hard	mpg	mpg	+20%
Average	+10%	+10%	+30%
Gentle		+20%	

	Regal 3/30 (701 cc)*	Robin 850 (848 cc)	Kitten Saloon	Kitten DL Estate
Maximum speed (mph)	71	77	78	76
Overall fuel consumption (mpg)	54.0	38.5	41.5	41.5
Fuel consumption (mpg) at constant:				
30 mph	–	–	75.5	80.0
50 mph	–	–	56.3	62.0
70 mph	–	–	37.4	48.0
Range on full fuel tank (miles)	324	231	249	249
Acceleration (seconds):				
0–30 mph	6.1	4.0	4.8	5.1
0–40 mph	10.8	6.4	8.1	9.0
0–50 mph	17.9	9.9	11.8	12.8
0–60 mph	31.1	16.1	19.6	20.2
0–70 mph	–	27.2	32.5	31.2
Standing start $\frac{1}{4}$ mile	23.0	19.7	21.2	21.3
40–60 mph in top gear	21.8	18.5	18.2	19.8

In the Driving Seat

Having taken a look at the family tree of the Regal, Robin and Kitten let's think about some of the more important things that you'll need to know from the driving seat. Fortunately, most of the controls are straightforward for the experienced motorist, but a little information on one or two points won't go amiss, particularly if you're not too familiar with Reliants.

Instruments and switches

The accompanying illustrations show typical instrument panel and control layouts for the various Reliant, Regal, Robin and Kitten models.

Ignition warning light (all models)

This warning light serves the dual purpose of reminding the driver that the ignition circuit is switched on (even though the engine may not be running), and acting as a no-charge indicator. The warning light should be on when the ignition's switched on, and may also be on when the engine's idling, but should go out at any speed above idling. If this doesn't happen, you've got a problem on your hands which needs looking into before you end up with a 'flat' (discharged) battery.

Oil pressure warning light (all models)

The oil pressure warning light should only come on when the ignition's switched on, and should go out as soon as the engine is running. If it doesn't go out within a second or so of start-up, the indication is that a considerable degree of wear exists somewhere in the engine mechanics, or (less likely) that some of the oil-ways are blocked. These faults can be lived with for a while, but expect problems in the future!

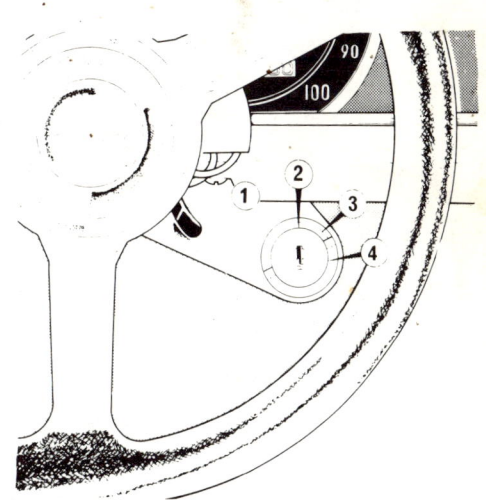

The ignition switch location and key positions (Robin models)

1 Auxiliaries on	3 Ignition on
2 Off	4 Starter

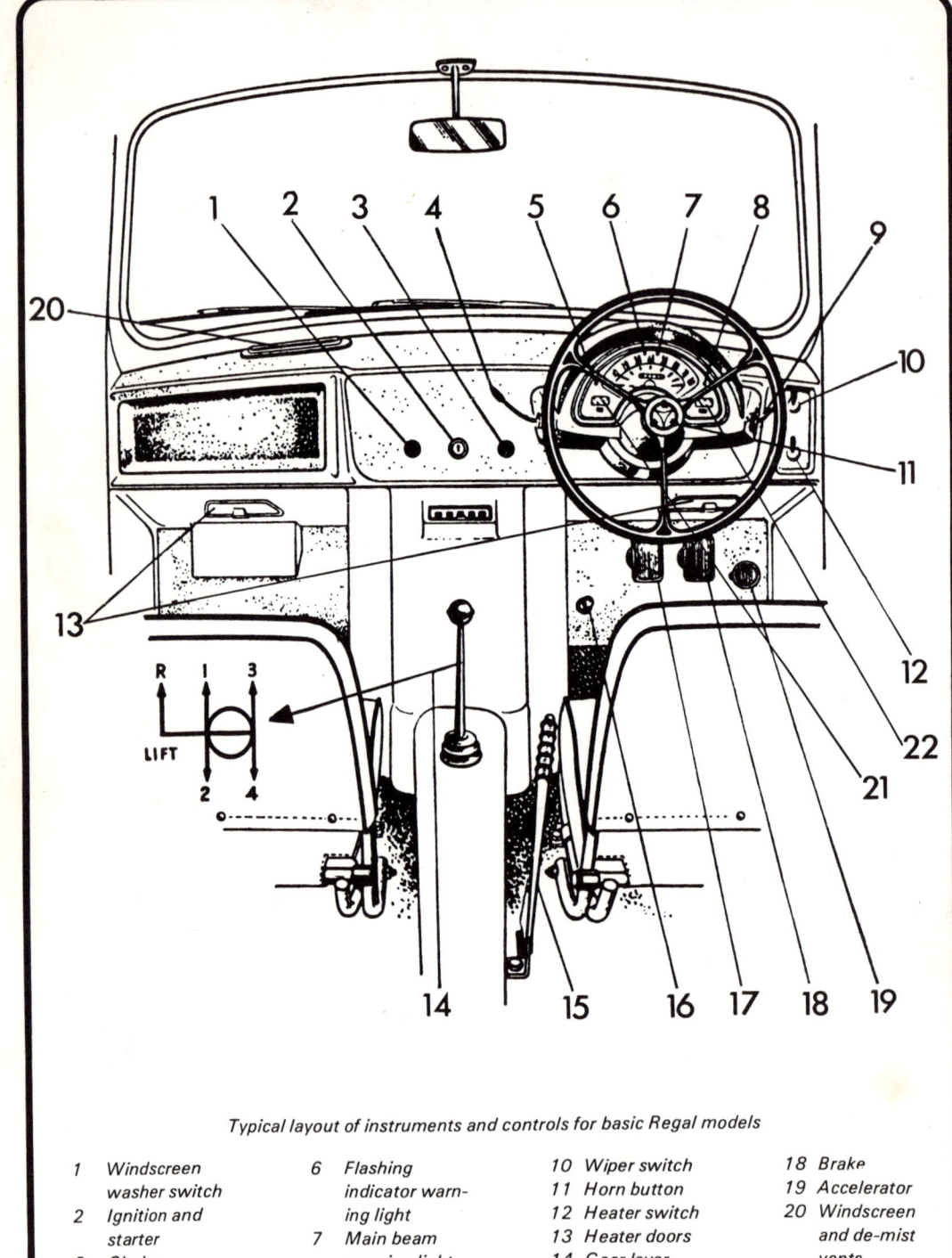

Typical layout of instruments and controls for basic Regal models

1 Windscreen washer switch	6 Flashing indicator warning light	10 Wiper switch	18 Brake
2 Ignition and starter	7 Main beam warning light	11 Horn button	19 Accelerator
3 Choke	8 Oil warning light	12 Heater switch	20 Windscreen and de-mist vents
4 Flasher switch		13 Heater doors	21 Fuel gauge
5 Ignition warning light	9 Lights switch	14 Gear lever	22 Temperature gauge
		15 Handbrake	
		16 Dipswitch	
		17 Clutch	

14

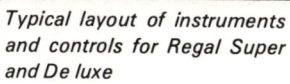

Typical layout of instruments and controls for Regal Super and De luxe

1 Windscreen washer control
2 Ignition/starter switch
3 Choke control
4 Direction indicator switch (later models)
5 Ignition warning light
6 Fuel gauge
7 Speedometer
8 Direction indicator warning light
9 Main-beam warning light
10 Horn button
11 Coolant temperature gauge
12 Oil pressure warning light
13 Light switch
14 Heater control (where fitted)
15 Windscreen wiper switch
16 Handbrake
17 Dip switch
18 Direction indicator switch (early models)

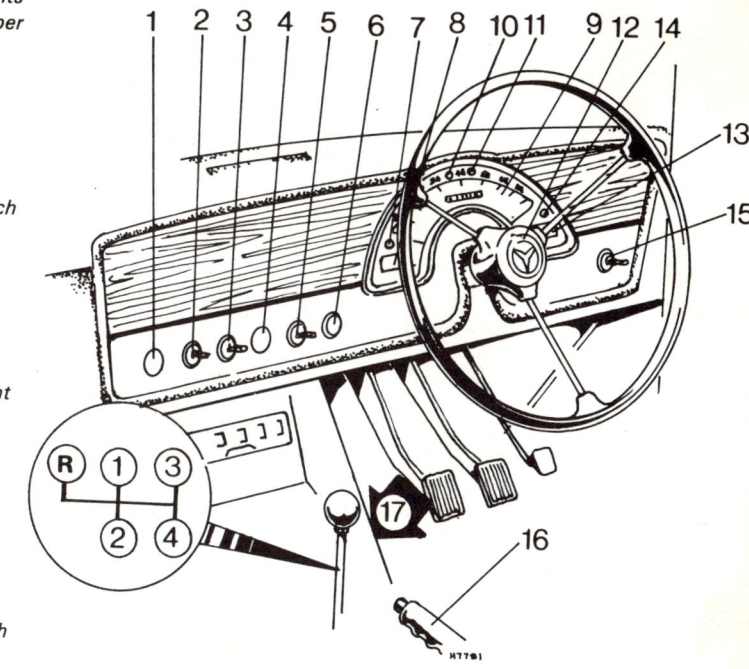

Instruments and controls as fitted to Robin models (typical layout)

1 Ignition switch
2 Multi-function switch
3 Auxiliary lights switch
4 Windscreen washer button
5 Hazard warning switch
6 Speedometer
7 Hazard warning indicator
8 Combined fuel and temperature gauge
9 Windscreen wiper switch
10 Lights switch
11 Heater fan switch
12 Heated rear screen switch
13 Oil pressure gauge
14 Fresh air vent
15 Battery condition indicator
16 Radio
17 Choke control
18 Heater control
19 Heater vent
20 Ash tray
21 Gear lever
22 Handbrake

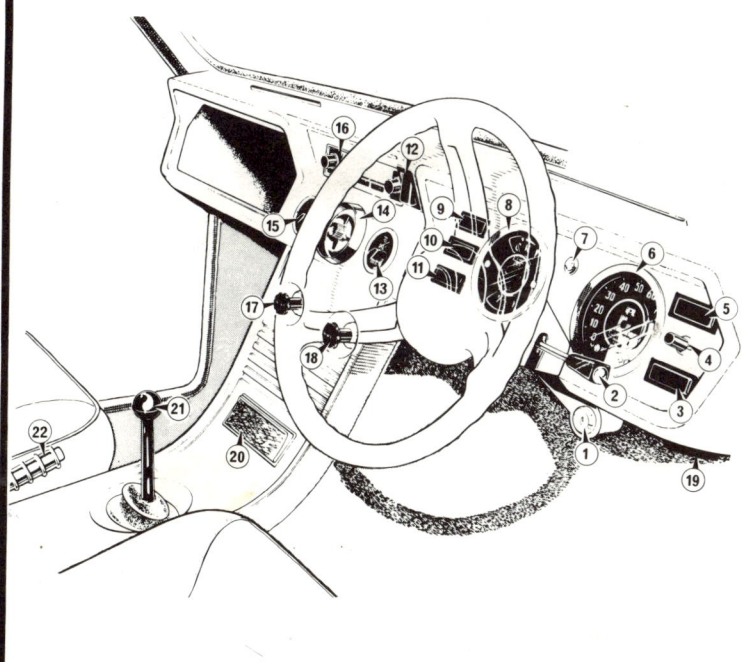

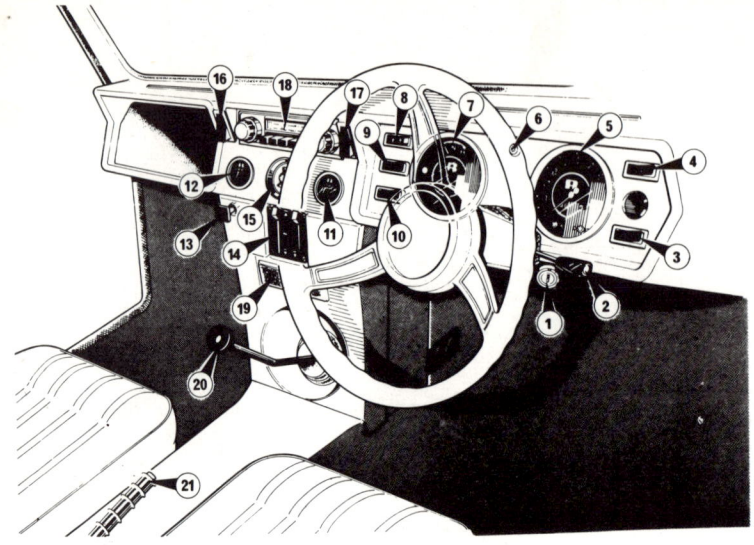

Typical layout of the instrument panel and controls of the Kitten range

1 Ignition/starter/
   steering lock
2 Multi-function
   switch
3 Auxiliary lights
   switch*
4 Hazard warning
   switch
5 Speedometer
6 Hazard warning

   indicator
7 Combined fuel
   and tempera-
   ture gauge
8 Heated rear
   screen switch
9 Lights switch
10 Heater fan
   switch

11 Oil pressure
   gauge*
12 Battery condi-
   tion indicator
13 Choke control
14 Heater control
   panel
15 Fresh air outlet
16 Rear wiper/

   washer switch
17 Windscreen
   wiper/washer
   switch
18 Radio
19 Ash tray
20 Gear lever
21 Handbrake
   lever

*Optional extras

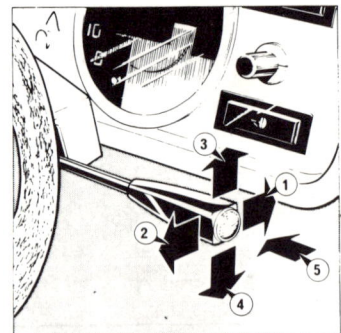

The combined ignition switch and steering column lock (Kitten models)

0 Steering locked – ignition off
1 Steering free – auxiliaries on
2 Ignition on
3 Starter

The various operating positions of the multi-function switch as fitted to Kitten and Robin models

1 Forward – headlamps on main beam
2 Back – headlamp flasher
3 Up – left-hand indicator
4 Down – right-hand indicator
5 Press – horn

16

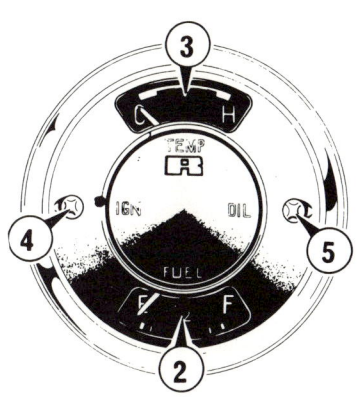

Details of the main instruments of the Kitten and Robin models

1 Speedometer	ture gauge	5 Oil pressure	warning light	8 Total mileage
2 Fuel gauge	4 Ignition warning	warning light	7 Main beam	recorder
3 Water tempera-	light	6 Indicator	warning light	

The heater control panel of the Kitten models

1 Air distribution control
2 Air temperature control

If the warning light comes on when you're travelling, expect trouble and **stop immediately**. It could be just a faulty warning light switch, but take a look at the engine oil dipstick - maybe you haven't checked the level lately and the engine's out of oil. If the oil level's OK get expert advice before driving any further.

Battery condition indicator (some Robin and Kitten models)

As the name suggests, this instrument will indicate the charged state of the battery. A reading of 12 volts indicates that the battery is in a reasonable charged condition, but if the gauge reads 11.5 volts or less the battery is in need of charging, which in turn may indicate either a faulty charging system or a faulty battery. When the gauge shows a reading in excess of 15 volts the battery is being over-charged and the cause should be investigated immediately or serious damage to other electrical components may result.

Oil pressure gauge (some Robin and Kitten models)

The oil pressure gauge gives a constant accurate indication of the engine oil pressure. It will be noticed that when the engine is started from cold the pressure gauge shows a high initial pressure, which will gradually fall off as the engine warms up. With the car travelling at approximately 40 mph and the engine operating at its normal working temperature the oil pressure gauge reading should be approximately 45 psi (3.16 kgf/cm^2). A very low gauge reading, or a failure to indicate any oil pressure, points directly to a serious problem which needs immediate investigation — see the remarks under 'Oil pressure warning light' above.

17

ADJUSTING SCREW

Front seat adjustment (Regal models)

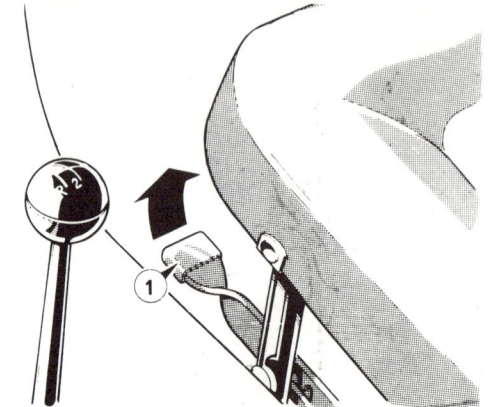

Front seat adjustment (Robin models). 1 – adjuster lever

Front seat adjustments (Kitten models)
A   Forwards and backwards
B   1   Seat release catch – lift to tilt seat
*   2   Reclining mechanism lever*

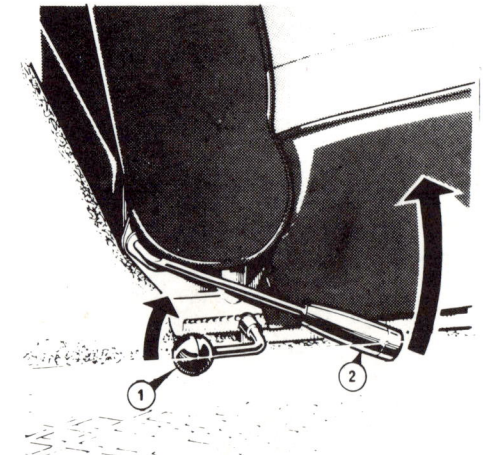

Rear seat catch (Robin and Kitten models) which must be released before the rear seat can be folded down
1   Rubber retaining strap
2   Seat rest bracket

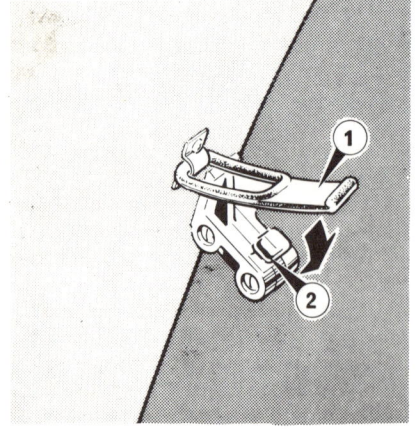

Rear seat folding procedure (Robin saloon model)
1   Seat cushion
2   Seat squab

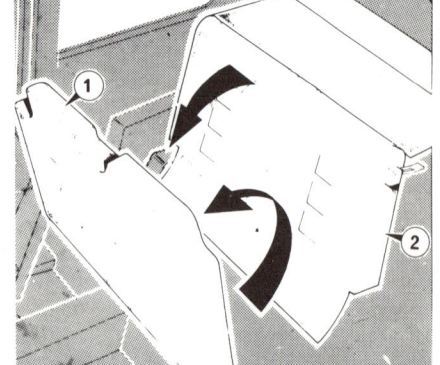

Rear seat folding procedure (Kitten estate model)

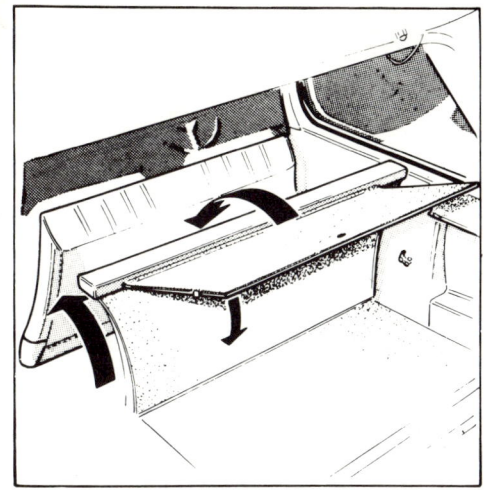

Rear seat folding procedure (Robin saloon model)

Switches

The switches on all Regal, Robin and Kitten models are laid out in a straightforward fashion which is clearly shown in the illustrations.

On Robin and Kitten models, the direction indicators, horn push, headlamp flasher and main/dip beam functions are all controlled by a single stalk projecting from the right-hand side of the steering column. Again, these functions are clearly shown in the accompanying illustration.

Driving the three-wheelers

Since 1963 it has been permissible for anyone with a valid motor-cycle driving licence, as well as a car licence, to drive a reversible three-wheeler, thus making it unnecessary for a motor-cyclist graduating to a Regal or Robin to take a further driving test.

For anyone used to driving a more conventional, four-wheeled car, although the controls of the three-wheelers are similar it may be found necessary to adapt one's driving technique somewhat.

It's perhaps stating the obvious to say that a car with only one wheel at the front cannot be quite as stable as its four-wheeled counterpart. You'll soon learn from experience, and the 'feel' of the car, what sort of cornering speeds are safe and how the car behaves under heavy braking. So if you're new to the three-wheel brigade, take it easy until you've found out exactly how your Regal or Robin handles.

Filling Station Facts

Forgetting about the actual servicing and maintenance for the time being, there are some things you'll need to know right from the very first day you get your Reliant. Then, assuming that the car was obtained as a going concern, you should be fit to drive around for a while to get the 'feel' of it. For anyone who's just acquired their car, or anyone who may be borrowing one, here's the absolute minimum of information required to get you up the road and back safely.

Tyre pressures

Note: Tyre pressures can only be checked accurately when the tyres are cold. Any tyre which has travelled more than a mile or so will have a pressure increase of several psi – perhaps more than 5 psi after a long run. Therefore, a certain amount of guesswork will be necessary if your tyres are warm. Since the pressures won't increase for any reason other than heat, the very least you can do is to set the front tyre(s) near to the correct pressure, and the two rear ones also (although front and rear pressures may not be the same), and we would expect these to be a little above the pressures shown in the tables.

If one tyre of a pair has a low pressure when warm, bring it up to the pressure of the other one on the same axle; if both are below the recommended cold pressure when warm, the safest thing to do is to bring them up to about 3 psi above the recommended 'cold' setting.

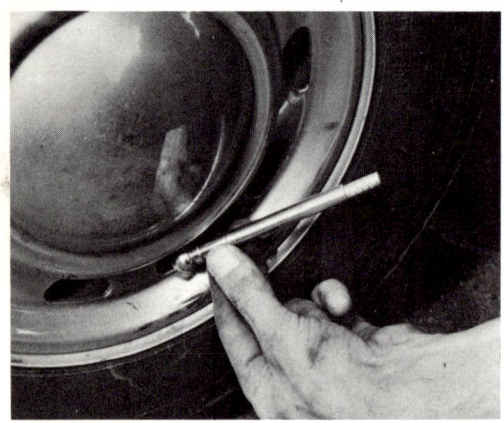

Checking the tyre pressures

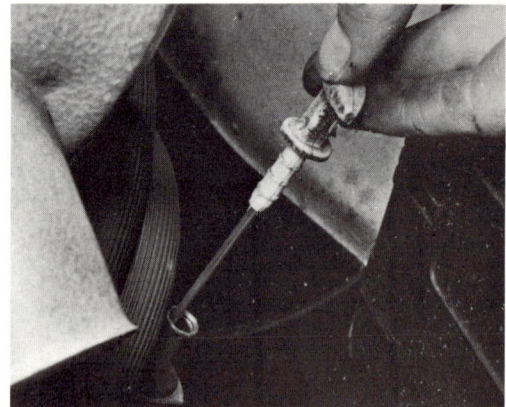

Removing the engine oil dipstick (Kitten model shown)

QUICK-CHECK CHART

TYRE PRESSURES   *Recommended pressures for cold tyres in psi (kgf/cm²)*

	Normal		Full load	
	Front	*Rear*	*Front*	*Rear*
Regal Saloon	18 (1.26)	20 (1.40)	18 (1.26)	24 (1.68)
Regal Van	20 (1.40)	24 (1.68)	20 (1.40)	30 (2.10)
Robin (all models)	30 (2.10)	24 (1.68)	30 (2.10)	30 (2.10)
Kitten (all models)	20 (1.40)	22 (1.54)	20 (1.40)	28 (1.96)

FUEL OCTANE RATING

All models (minimum)   95 octane (3 star)

Note: If 'pinking' is experienced with Kitten models use 97 octane (4 star)

FUEL TANK CAPACITY

All models   6 gallons (27.27 litres)

ENGINE OIL TYPE

All models   20W/50 multigrade

QUANTITY OF OIL REQUIRED TO BRING LEVEL FROM *MIN* TO *MAX* ON DIPSTICK

All models   1.25 pints (0.71 litre)

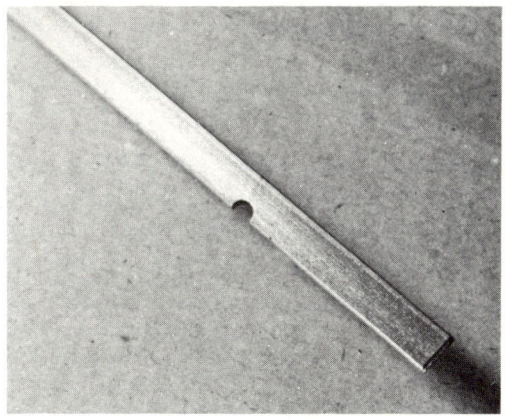

The cut-out on the dipstick represents the 'full' mark (Kitten model shown)

In An Emergency

There's no car yet invented that can guarantee to give you a safe and reliable journey from point A to point B every day of your life. Be it due to a breakdown or a puncture, the day will come when your trusty transport requires a bit of roadside attention - usually at the most inconvenient time. In this Handbook you'll find a wealth of information which should certainly minimize the possibility of a breakdown but, although we trust it won't be very often, the odd thing's bound to go wrong from time to time.

The Troubleshooting Section should help you to locate the source of an unexpected problem, but it's of little advantage knowing what's wrong if you've nothing to put it right with, or needing to change a wheel in the dark when you haven't a clue how the jack works. A few timely minutes spent reading through these pages now could save you time and temper later on!

Spares and repairs kit

The basic tool kit supplied with your Reliant won't get you very far should you have the misfortune of a roadside breakdown. An additional tool kit is a wise precaution – for further information see *Tools for the Job*.

A few items which can be used or fitted without too much bother at the roadside should also be carried. These can prove invaluable in getting you out of trouble on the odd occasion when they might be needed. The sort of things you should carry are:

Spark plugs, properly cleaned and gapped
HT lead and plug cap – one that will reach the furthest plug from the distributor
Set of light bulbs
Fuses
Distributor, rotor, condenser and contact breaker set
Fan belt
Roll of insulating tape

Tin of radiator sealer
First aid box and manual
Spare set of keys (but not in the car)
Extension light and lead with crocodile clips
Windscreen de-icer aerosol (during winter months)
Breakdown triangle
Tow rope
Clean lint-free cloth
This Handbook

Jacking up and wheel changing

The scissor-type jack supplied with your Reliant is suitable for changing a wheel by the roadside, and that's about all. If the car is to be jacked up for any other reason, a stronger and more reliable means of support will be required; for further information on this, refer to *Tools for the Job*.

As already mentioned, all models are equipped with a scissor type jack which is stowed with the spare wheel and tool kit at the rear of the vehicle.

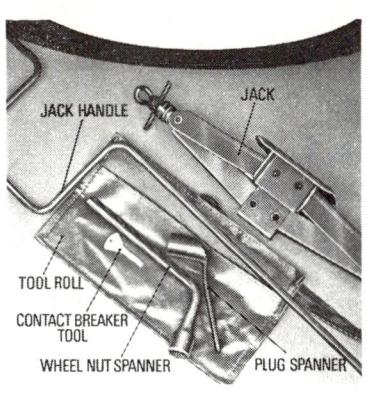

The basic tool kit which every Regal model was supplied with

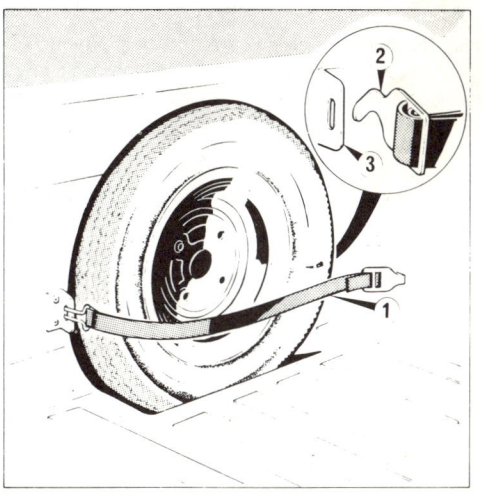

The spare wheel location and fixing (Robin saloon model)
1 retaining strap   2 hook   3 bracket

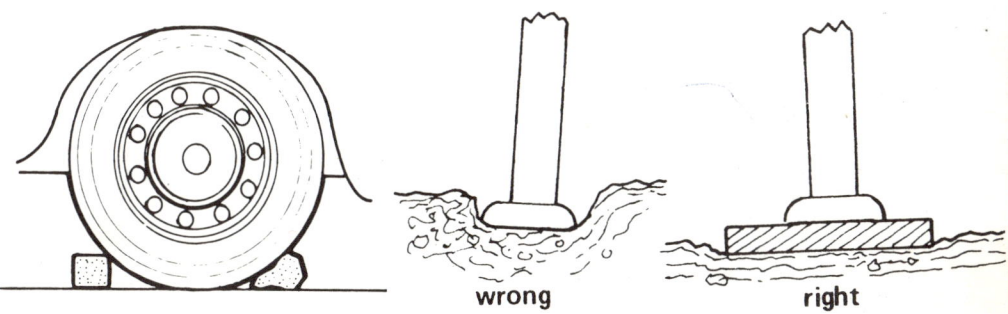

Always wedge the wheels before jacking.

Spread the load under the foot of the jack

Slackening the wheelnuts prior to jacking the car up

Location of the spare wheel (Kitten saloon model)

Various locations and fixings are provided depending on the particular model type but we've included a few typical illustrations. The scissor jack is designed to lift the vehicle at specific points along the main chassis frame as shown in the other relevant accompanying illustrations.

To commence the wheel changing operation, first apply the handbrake and engine first gear. Now remove the spare wheel, wheel brace and jack from their stowage places at the rear of the car. Where hub caps are fitted, lever them off using the end of the jack handle or a large screwdriver, but take care when doing this as the paintwork and hub cap can easily be damaged. Using the wheel brace slacken, but don't remove, the wheel nuts (they undo in an anti-clockwise direction). Hopefully the wheelnuts won't be too tight, but if they are a bit of footpower on the brace may be required.

Now find something to chock one of the wheels which is to remain on the ground. An old brick or block of wood is just the job, but unless you carry such a thing you may have to improvise. If you can only find one, weigh up which way the vehicle is likely to move if anything goes wrong; hopefully you'll find two, then one can be put each side of a wheel.

The scissor jack can now be placed in the correct position (see illustrations) under the main chassis frame. Locate the hooked eye of the jack handle in the end of the jack and turn the handle in a clockwise direction until the road wheel is well clear of the ground. Remove the four wheel nuts followed by the wheel. The spare wheel can now be fitted in position and the wheel nuts nipped up.

Don't try to fully tighten the wheel nuts with the car jacked up as you may cause the vehicle to rock and topple off the jack. Lower the jack, by turning the handle in an anti-clockwise direction, and then tighten the wheel nuts evenly in a cross-wise order. You don't have to stand on the wheelbrace or use a length of piping to increase the leverage but in the interests of safety it's essential to ensure that the wheel nuts are good and tight. In case you're interested the correct wheel tightening torque setting is 30 to 35 lbf ft (4.15 to 4.84 kgf m).

Where a hub cap is used this can now be refitted, by holding it in position over all but one of the retaining lugs and hitting it smartly with the ball of your hand to spring it over the remaining one. Finally secure the punctured wheel, jack and wheelbrace in the stowage at the rear of the vehicle and remove the wheel chocks.

Hopefully (and if you're following the correct maintenance procedures, there should be no problem) the spare wheel will have the correct pressure in it. If you're not sure, drive carefully until it can be checked. And don't forget to have the punctured tyre mended (or in extreme cases, renewed) as soon as possible.

Light bulb renewal

Sealed beam unit (Regal and Robin models)

First remove the outer chrome ring. On Regal models this is retained by a single self-tapping screw and several protruding lugs on the headlamp inner shell. Robin models do not have a retaining screw at the base of the outer ring and rely solely on the protruding lugs to retain the ring. Remove the self-tapping screw (where applicable) and carefully prise off the outer ring using a screwdriver.

An inner ring retains the sealed beam unit in position and is itself held in position by three self-tapping screws. Remove the three screws and inner ring and lift the sealed beam unit out far enough to allow the three-pin connector to be disconnected from the rear of the unit.

Fitting the new sealed beam unit is the reverse of the removal procedure but some difficulty may be experienced when trying to refit the outer ring. The simplest method is to fit the ring at the top in such a way that it's located over the upper protruding lugs, then press the lower part of the rim firmly inwards using both hands so that it springs over the remaining lugs. Remember, on Regal models it's essential to make sure that the retaining screw hole in the ring is correctly aligned with the captive nut fitted to the inner headlamp shell.

Headlamp bulb/sealed beam unit (Kitten models)

Remove the front grille panel which is retained by several self-tapping screws. The headlamp unit is held in position by a retainer ring and four self-tapping screws. Remove the screws and retainer, lift out the headlamp unit and pull off the three-pin wiring connector. Where a sealed beam unit is fitted simply fit the new unit. Where the headlamp has a bulb, spring back the retainer clips and lift out the bulb. Reverse the removal sequence for refitting.

Headlamp bulb (Super Robin models)

Some Robin models are fitted with quartz-halogen headlamp bulbs which are superior to the ordinary sealed beam type. Remove the headlamp outer and inner rings as described above for other Robin models. Lift the headlamp unit out and disconnect the wiring connections at the rear of the headlamp unit. The bulb is located in the reflector with a spring clip.

Note: When handling quartz-halogen bulbs it's essential to avoid touching any part of the glass envelope, so hold the bulb by its base. If by chance

The scissor jack correctly positioned when raising a rear wheel

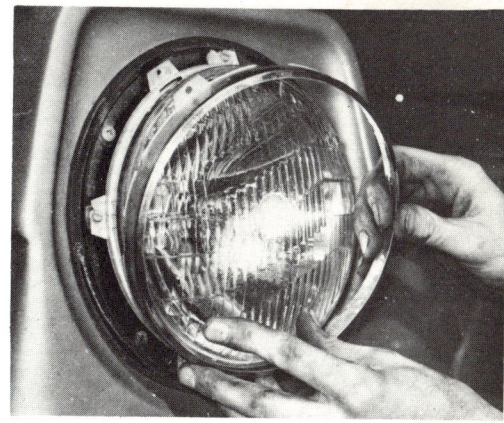

Removing the outer chrome retainer ring (Regal model shown)

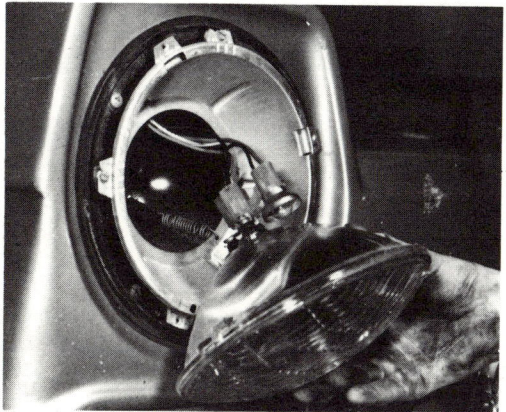

Lifting away the sealed beam unit (Regal model shown)

Removing the front grille panel (Kitten model)

Remove the retainer ring and lift out the headlamp unit (Kitten model)

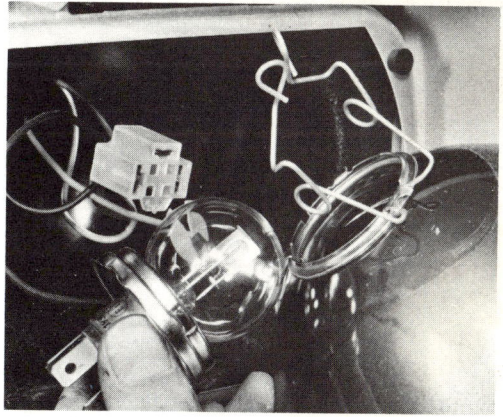

Removing the headlamp bulb (Kitten model)

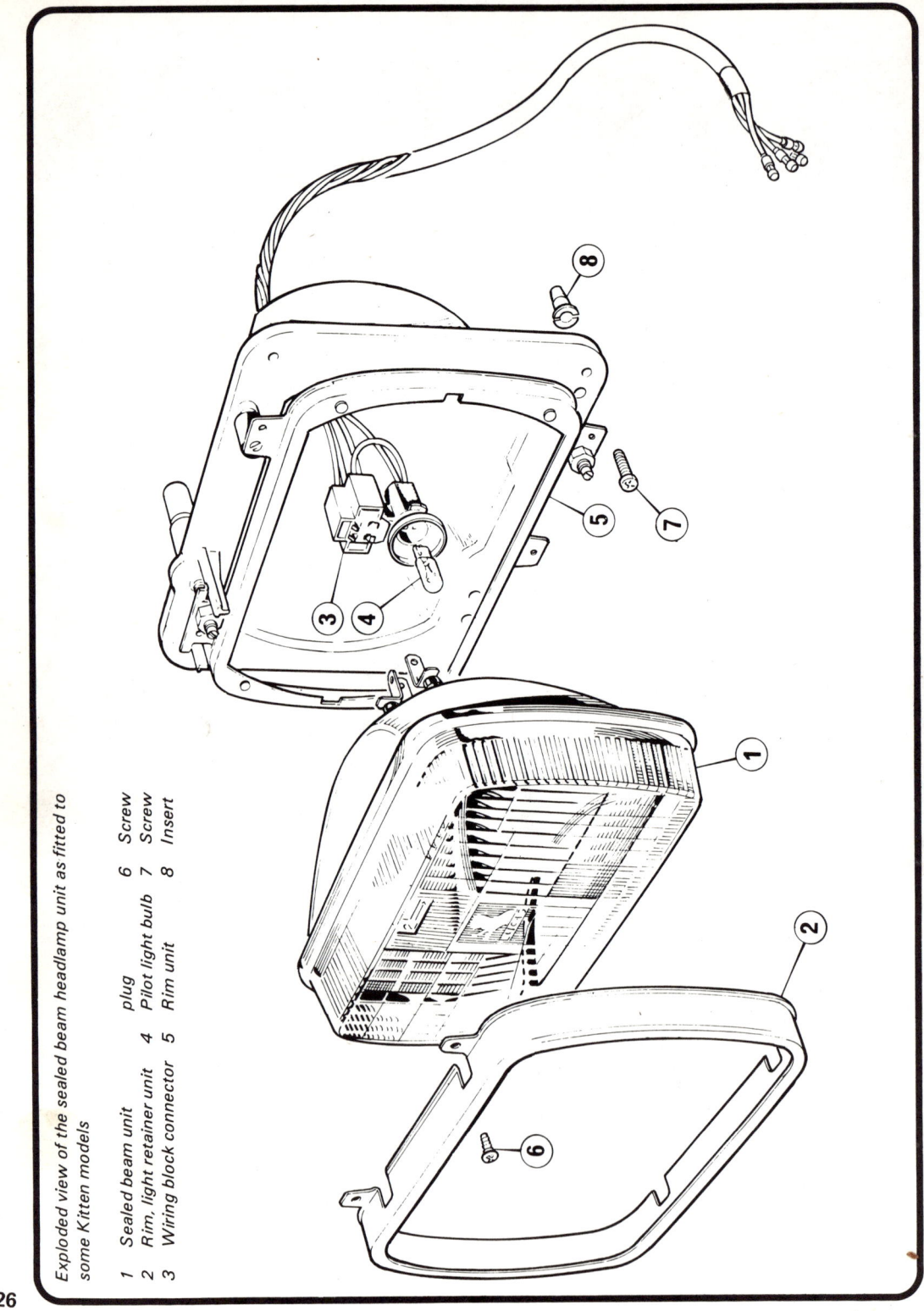

Exploded view of the sealed beam headlamp unit as fitted to some Kitten models

1 Sealed beam unit
2 Rim, light retainer unit
3 Wiring block connector

4 plug
  Pilot light bulb
5 Rim unit

6 Screw
7 Screw
8 Insert

you happen to touch the glass, the bulb must be cleaned immediately with methylated spirits and a soft rag or the efficiency of the lamp will be greatly reduced. Refitting the headlamp assembly is the reverse of the removal procedure.

Front side/indicator lamp bulb (Regal models)

Early Regal models have separate front side and indicator lamps while later ones have a combined single side/indicator lamp. Bulb replacement is identical but the bulb type is different and depends on the type of lamp (s) fitted (See *Vital Statistics* for further details).

To remove the lens insert a screwdriver under the lip of the rubber flange and prise out the chrome ring and the lens. The bulb fitted to this type of lamp is of the bayonet 'push-twist' type and is simple to remove and fit provided that the bulb holder isn't corroded.

Front side (pilot) lamp bulb (Kitten and Robin models)

The side (pilot) lamps of these models are fitted behind the headlamp units. Access to the bulb holders can only be achieved by removing the headlamps (refer to 'Headlamp' section above for details).

Kitten and Robin models with sealed beam headlamp units have side (pilot) lamp bulb holders which are fitted with 'capless' bulbs of the 'push-fit' type. Super Robin models with quartz halogen bulb type headlamps have side (pilot) lamps which are fitted into the headlamp reflector unit, the bulbs of which are of the bayonet 'push twist' type.

Front direction indicator bulb (Kitten and Robin models)

Remove the two lens retaining screws and lift away the lens. The bulb fitted to this lamp is of the bayonet 'push-twist' type. When refitting the lens avoid overtightening the retaining screws or damage may result to the lens.

Stop/tail and direction indicator bulbs (Kitten and Robin models)

Access to the bulbs can be gained after removing the rear light lens which is retained by two screws. The bulbs fitted are of the regular bayonet 'push-twist' type.

Stop/tail and direction indicator bulbs (Regal models)

Access to the bulbs can be achieved from the rear of the lamp. Unscrew the central bulb holder retainer screw and lift away the bulb holder. The bulbs fitted to these lamps are of the bayonet 'push-twist' type.

Removing the front direction indicator lens (Regal 21-E model shown)

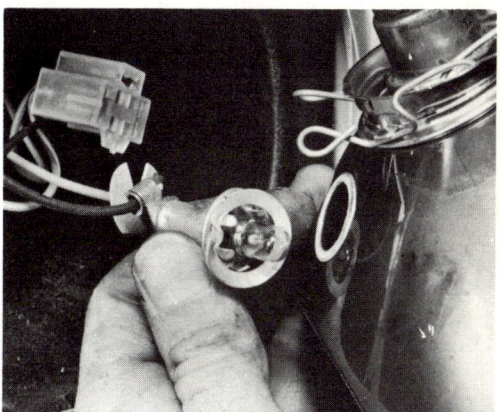

Removing the pilot lamp bulb holder (Kitten and Robin models)

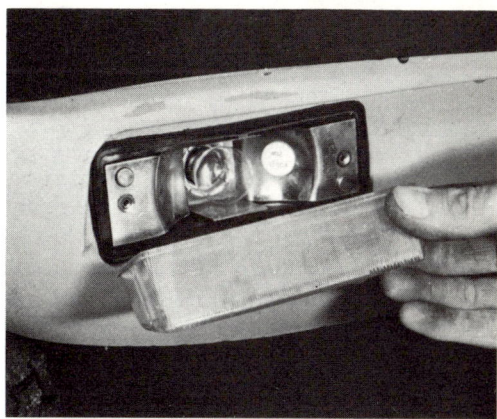

Removing the front direction indicator lens (Kitten and Robin models)

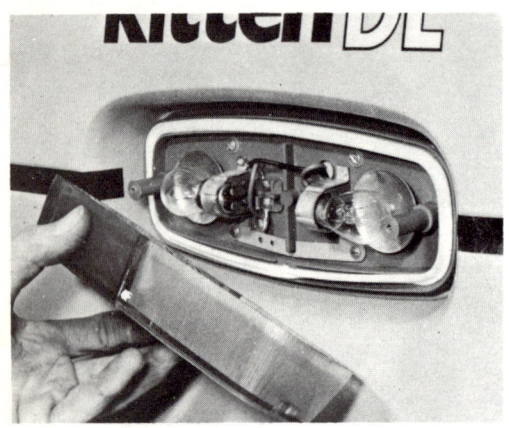

Removing the rear lamp lens (Kitten model shown)

Removing the rear lamp assembly bulb holders (Regal model)

The number plate lamp assembly shown dismantled (all models)

The fuse box with cover removed (Kitten model shown)

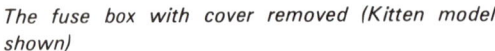

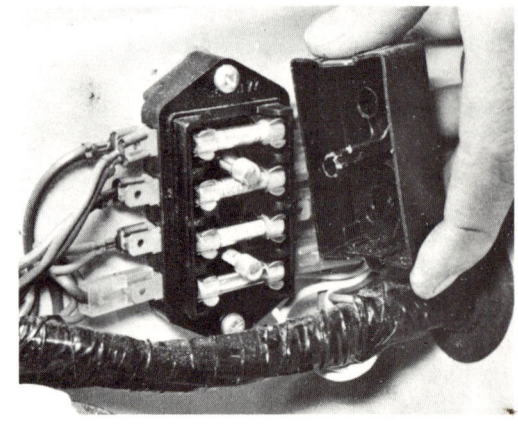

Number plate lamp bulb (all models)

To renew the number plate lamp bulb, first remove the two screws securing the chrome bezel in position. Lift off the bezel and lens to gain access to the bayonet type bulb.

Interior light bulb (all models)

Squeeze together the sides of the plastic cover lens sufficiently to release the lens from the main light assembly. The bulb fitted to this light is of the tubular festoon type which is held in position between two spring contact plates.

Ignition warning lamp/direction indicator warning lamp and headlamp main beam warning light bulbs (all models)

To renew any of these bulbs, reach up behind the instrument panel and pull out the respective bulb holder from its mounting point. With the bulb holder now released it's a straightforward operation to renew the faulty bulb.

Hazard warning light bulb (Kitten and Robin models)

This warning lamp is mounted in a central position between the two main instruments. The bulb holder can be prised out of the lamp lens from behind the instrument panel. Remove the faulty bulb from the holder and fit the replacement. Reassembly of the components is the reverse of the removal procedure.

Heated rear window switch warning lamp bulb (Kitten and Robin models)

The warning lamp is an integral part of the switch. To renew the warning lamp bulb, carefully lever the switch away from the facia panel whilst depressing the two retainer lugs which are a part of the switch body. Now remove the faulty bulb and fit the replacement. Reassembly of the components is the reverse of the removal procedure.

Fuses - location and renewal

Fuses are incorporated as safety 'weak links' in various electrical circuits (see *Vital Statistics* for individual details) to prevent serious damage due to a 'short circuit' or similar fault. Fuses are individually rated and if one should 'blow' you'll have to find the reason why it 'blew' before fitting a new one. Never replace a 'blown' fuse with one of a higher rating or be tempted to use a piece of tin foil as a substitute - you'll simply be defeating the object of having a fuse in the first place and you'll probably end up with a more serious fault at the end.

The fuses are housed in a fuse box which is located on the right-hand bulkhead in the engine compartment just above the brake master cylinder (Kitten and Robin models) or below the ignition coil (Regal models). To renew a fuse, simply pull off the fuse box cover and remove the faulty fuse. Fit the new fuse and refit the cover.

Save It!

Do-it-yourself car servicing is all about saving money, but never forget that you're striving to maintain your car in a reliable and safe state, so money saving should always be considered as secondary to safety standards. The following pages are all about cost cutting in simple, practical ways, which may be obvious, but perhaps you've never really thought about it in these terms before.

Tyres

Without any doubt whatsoever, a radial tyre will give you much better value for money than a crossply because, although it will initially be somewhat dearer, it will last a great deal longer. Remould tyres can give good service, but they have their limitations when used for family motoring; remould radials now have a more reliable reputation than they had when they first appeared on the market, but sometimes give a bit of trouble when trying to balance them.

So, what have we learnt so far? Only that you 'pays your money and takes your choice'. In the broadest terms, the more you pay for a tyre, the better value for money you get. If you're after the best in roadholding and tyre life, buy radials; if you want good tyre life, and aren't quite so worried about the roadholding under adverse conditions, buy crossplies; if you want a good runabout tyre, and aren't thinking of high speeds or long journeys, buy radial remoulds but they may give a little steering wheel 'shimmy' if used on the front; if you want the cheapest tyre which still complies with the law in safety standards, buy remould crossplies.

Regrade tyres are sometimes available (they used to be known as remould quality or RQ); these are tyres which may have the very slightest of defects in the tread pattern or moulding, but are otherwise perfect. If you get the chance to buy these, buy them – to all intents and purposes they're as good as a new tyre.

It's not generally realised that the major tyre manufacturers also produce tyres under less well-known names at somewhat cheaper prices. These are first-class buys also – ask any dealer.

One last point with tyres – keep them properly inflated; this improves tyre life and reduces rolling resistance. **Note:** Reliant do not recommend that Regal or Robin models are fitted with radial ply tyres, but if you want to fit them, do so on all three wheels.

Batteries

Like tyres, batteries have become a specialist sales area. Don't be misled into thinking that all batteries are the same and buy the cheapest one available just to save money.

Generally speaking the price and quality of the battery go hand in hand, but aren't always directly proportional. All batteries are guaranteed and should last for the guarantee period and a bit longer, but they always seem to 'pack up' at the most inconvenient time. When buying a battery try to get one with a two or three year guarantee – it'll be worthwhile and it needn't be the dearest one around.

A final word on battery care – if you look after your battery it'll look after you. Battery care is covered in *Service Scene*.

Lubricants

Very cheap engine oils are on sale but you can never be certain which are good and which are to be avoided, so it's best to steer clear of them.

Do-it-yourself motoring and accessory shops stock many makes of good quality multigrade engine oils. The large 5 litre (they used to be 1 gallon) cans are large enough for most purposes, and contain enough for an engine oil change with a surplus for topping-up purposes.

Unless you're forced to, never buy oil in pint or half litre cans, this is the most expensive way of buying oil, especially from filling stations. You can, incidentally, purchase oil from wholesalers, in large drums and save even more money. These drums need to be fitted with a tap for easy dispensing.

Anti-freeze can be purchased in bulk but you never need to buy it in such large quantities. Motoring and accessory shops are usually the best bet when you need any.

Greases, brake fluid, etc are best purchased from the motoring shops, as again you never need to purchase large quantities – but make sure you buy something that's good quality and (in the case of anti-freeze) is suitable for the all-aluminium engine of your Reliant.

Fuel

The grade of fuel (usually given an octane/star rating) which you use in your Reliant is important. Don't be misled into thinking that you'll get an increase in performance by filling your tank with fuel of a higher rating – you won't, you're simply wasting your money. Similarly, don't think you'll be saving money by using a lower grade fuel, your engine's performance (and probably your engine too) will suffer.

You may, one day have no option but to buy a lower grade fuel, perhaps if the garage has run out of your particular grade, and in these circumstances, drive carefully until you can get the correct grade; it may be beneficial to retard the ignition by a few degrees but then you've got the fuss of resetting it again later.

Engine tuning

This is one of the most misused terms in use today; it really means getting the best in terms of economy and performance from your car. Generally its found that in the search for increased performance fuel economy drops and vice versa. It's very difficult

and expensive to improve on the specifications and settings which the manufacturer has laid down for your Reliant. Reliant have invested a great deal of time and money in their products to obtain the ultimate settings whilst still retaining a high degree of reliability from the mechanical parts of their vehicles.

Many of the so-called economy devices you see advertised claim to increase performance, ease starting and save fuel into the bargain. If these claims were fully justified don't you think that Reliant would have fitted the devices to their cars? Before you consider fitting such a device it's best to seek the advice of a Reliant owner who has fitted and tried one; in this way you'll find out if it really works without having to spend any money.

The cheapest and most effective method of keeping your car in a good state of tune is undoubtedly regular maintenance (e.g. spark plugs, distributor points, ignition timing, carburettor adjustments and valve clearances). If you ensure that these are regularly attended to, the rest is up to you.

Driving habits

If you've taken the trouble to ensure that your car is in a decent state of tune, why spoil it by the way you drive? Many drivers have bad habits which only waste petrol and wear out the mechanical parts prematurely. 'Blipping' the throttle at traffic lights, for example, and when they change to green engaging the clutch fiercely to obtain a speedy getaway. Have you ever stopped to consider what this can do to fuel consumption figures and the enormous strain it puts on the transmission system?

The true skill in economical driving is using the pedals sensibly. There's simply no need to race the engine or to engage the clutch fiercely when pulling away; a moderate engine speed, and careful engagement of the clutch, will produce the same end result with greater fuel economy.

When you're on the move, try leaving the throttle pedal in the same position while the car accelerates – you may need to press it down a little further but don't press it too hard, there just isn't the need for it. The time you've saved while accelerating rapidly will be lost next time you refill your fuel tank.

Some owners fit a vacuum gauge (sometimes called a performance gauge) to their cars, which through a tapping point in the inlet manifold registers the inlet manifold vacuum. The art of driving using the vacuum gauge is to keep the gauge needle on a high vacuum reading. Wide throttle openings represent a low vacuum reading, so you can adjust your throttle pedal position to gain maximum economy under all operating conditions. You'll soon get used to knowing when to ease off your right foot pressure, and when you can apply it and still keep the gauge needle on a **31** high vacuum reading.

Roof racks

The ever faithful roof rack has proved a boon to so many motorists for the extra holiday luggage, but how often do you see cars being driven around with an empty roof rack still attached? Many estimates have been made of the increase in fuel consumption caused by a roof rack due to wind resistance, and the generally accepted figure is around 10%, with a loaded rack, this figure can be be as high as 30%. The moral, then, is obvious – don't use a roof rack unless you have to, and always remove it when it's not in use.

Insurance

Like some of the other things that we've discussed, the service you're going to get from your insurance company will be related to the cost of the cover obtained. A cheap policy's good until you need to make a claim, and then the sort of snags you're going to come across are 'How do I get hold of an assessor to inspect the damage...?' or 'How will it affect my No Claims Bonus...?'

There are one or two legitimate ways of reducing the policy premium, perhaps by insuring for 'owner/driver only', 'two named drivers', or an agreement to pay the first £20 or so of any claim. Many large companies have a discount scheme for their employees if they use the same insurance company; this also applies to bank and Civil Service employees. You may also get a better bargain by insuring through one of the Motoring Associations if you're a member.

What it all adds up to is (1) Insure well; (2) See what you can get in the way of discounts; and (3) Find out exactly what you're covered for.

Buying spare parts

There aren't very many parts which will either outlast, or give better service than, the genuine spares manufactured or marketed by Reliant. One notable exception is the stainless steel exhaust system which will last almost indefinitely. There is one drawback however – the cost of a stainless steel system is considerably more than that of a regular mild steel system. If you're intending to keep your Reliant for more than 3 or 4 years the fitting of such a system could well be worthwhile, so consider these points when you've got to buy a new exhaust.

When it comes to servicing you know that you're going to need oils and grease, but sooner or later you'll have to buy some other parts too. Smaller items, e.g. spark plugs, fan belts, oil filters etc, can easily be obtained, but larger, less common items can be difficult to locate. The sort of places where you can buy new/service exchange parts when they're required are:

Officially appointed Reliant dealers: Your local Reliant dealer should be able to get you any parts which you may require, but there's often a drawback as these parts are generally dearer than those purchased from other sales outlets. The parts your local Reliant dealer sells are genuine Reliant 'R' parts which have been manufactured by Reliant and should be superior in quality to other manufacturers' replica parts, so you'll know that the Reliant manufactured parts will fit without any snags.

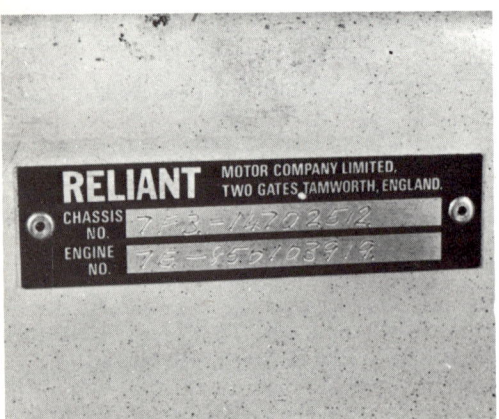

The vehicle identification plate showing chassis and engine numbers

The engine number is also stamped on the cylinder block casting

Other garages and accessory shops: These are usually the best places from which to get such items as oil filters, fan belts, contact sets etc — the very parts that you're likely to need when carrying out your own servicing and maintenance. Remember that general accessories can often be purchased at these places also. The advantage of buying your bits and pieces here is the lower prices and the convenient opening hours, whilst not forgetting the fact that these sales outlets may be quite close to your home.

Some of the leading car manufacturers produce a wide range of general spare parts to suit the vehicles manufactured by their competitors. Chrysler produce spare parts under the 'Mopar' brand name, British Leyland use the 'Unipart' name and Ford produce the 'Motorcraft' spare parts range, so you should have no problems obtaining the odd part or two when it's required.

Motor Factors: Good factors will sell all the larger, more important components you'll need for the engine, gearbox, suspension and braking systems. Many of these items are sold on an exchange basis and are also guaranteed for a period of time.

If you're obtaining a part through a service exchange scheme, make sure that the part you're returning is clean and check it against the service exchange part to ensure that it's the same.

Vehicle identification numbers

When you're buying new parts the partsman will need to know certain information about your car. The very least he'll need to know is the make, model and year of manufacture. For some parts he'll have to be told the car's engine number, and maybe the chassis number (which you always meant to take a note of but never got round to doing it!). Why not take a note of these now in your pocket diary or perhaps the inside cover of this Handbook?

The vehicle identification plate is mounted in the engine compartment and shows clearly the chassis number and the engine number; a typical example is shown in the accompanying photograph. The engine number's also stamped on to the cylinder block casting on the right-hand side, just below the cylinder head, at the rear of the engine.

Vital Statistics

At some time or other you'll need to know, or refer to, the following information which is applicable to your particular Reliant model. We'll start at the engine specifications and work our way through all the essential parts ...

ENGINE

Type	4 cylinder overhead valve, pushrod operated
Capacity	
Regal models, 1962 to 1968 (Aug)	598 cc
Regal models 1968 (Aug) onwards	701 cc
Robin models 1973 (Oct) to 1975 (Nov)	748 cc
Later Robin and all Kitten models	848 cc

Bore	
598 cc	55.88 mm (2.2 in)
701 cc	60.5 mm (2.38 in)
748 cc	62.5 mm (2.46 in)
848 cc	62.5 mm (2.46 in)

Stroke	
598 cc	60.96 mm (2.4 in)
701 cc	60.96 mm (2.4 in)
748 cc	60.96 mm (2.4 in)
848 cc	69.09 mm (2.72 in)

Compression ratio (standard)	
598 cc	7.8 : 1
701 cc	7.3 : 1
748 cc	7.5 : 1
848 cc	9.5 : 1

Firing order	
All models	1, 3, 4, 2 (No 1 cylinder nearest radiator)

A sectional view of the 850 cc engine fitted to the Robin and Kitten models

VITAL STATISTICS

Idling speed	refer to Fuel System data

Valve clearances:

All models, inlet and exhaust (hot)	0.010 in
(cold)	0.006 in

Maximum power output (bhp)

598 cc	26 @ 5000 rpm
701 cc	29 @ 5000 rpm
748 cc	32 @ 5500 rpm
848 cc	40 @ 5500 rpm

Maximum torque output (lbf ft)

598 cc	29 @ 3100 rpm
701 cc	34.6 @ 3000 rpm
748 cc	36.5 @ 3000 rpm
848 cc	46 @ 3500 rpm

Lubrication system

Oil pump type	eccentric rotor
Oil pressure (normal):	
598, 701 and 748 cc engines	30 to 35 lbf/in^2
848 cc engine	45 lbf/in^2
Oil filter	full-flow type
Oil type	20W/50 multigrade type (for normal UK operating conditions)

Sump capacity (including filter)

598 and 701 cc engines	5.0 Imp. pints (2.8 litres)
748 and 848 cc engines	5.5 Imp. pints (3.13 litres)

COOLING SYSTEM

System type	pressurised with belt-driven water pump and cooling fan

Thermostat

Type	wax
Opening temperature (start):	
598 and 701 cc engines	80°C (176°F)
848 cc engine	86° to 89°C (187° to 193°F)
Fully open temperature:	
598 and 701 cc engines	94°C (200°F)
848 cc engine	103°C (218°F)

Pressure cap release pressure

598 and 701 cc engines	4 lbf/in^2
848 cc engine	7 lbf/in^2

Fan belt tension	0.5 in (13 mm) deflection at midpoint of belt between generator and water pump pulleys

System capacity (including heater)

Regal models	7.0 pints (4 litres)
Robin models	5.0 pints (2.84 litres)
Kitten models	6.5 pints (3.69 litres)

36 *Antifreeze type*	ethylene glycol with corrosion inhibitors

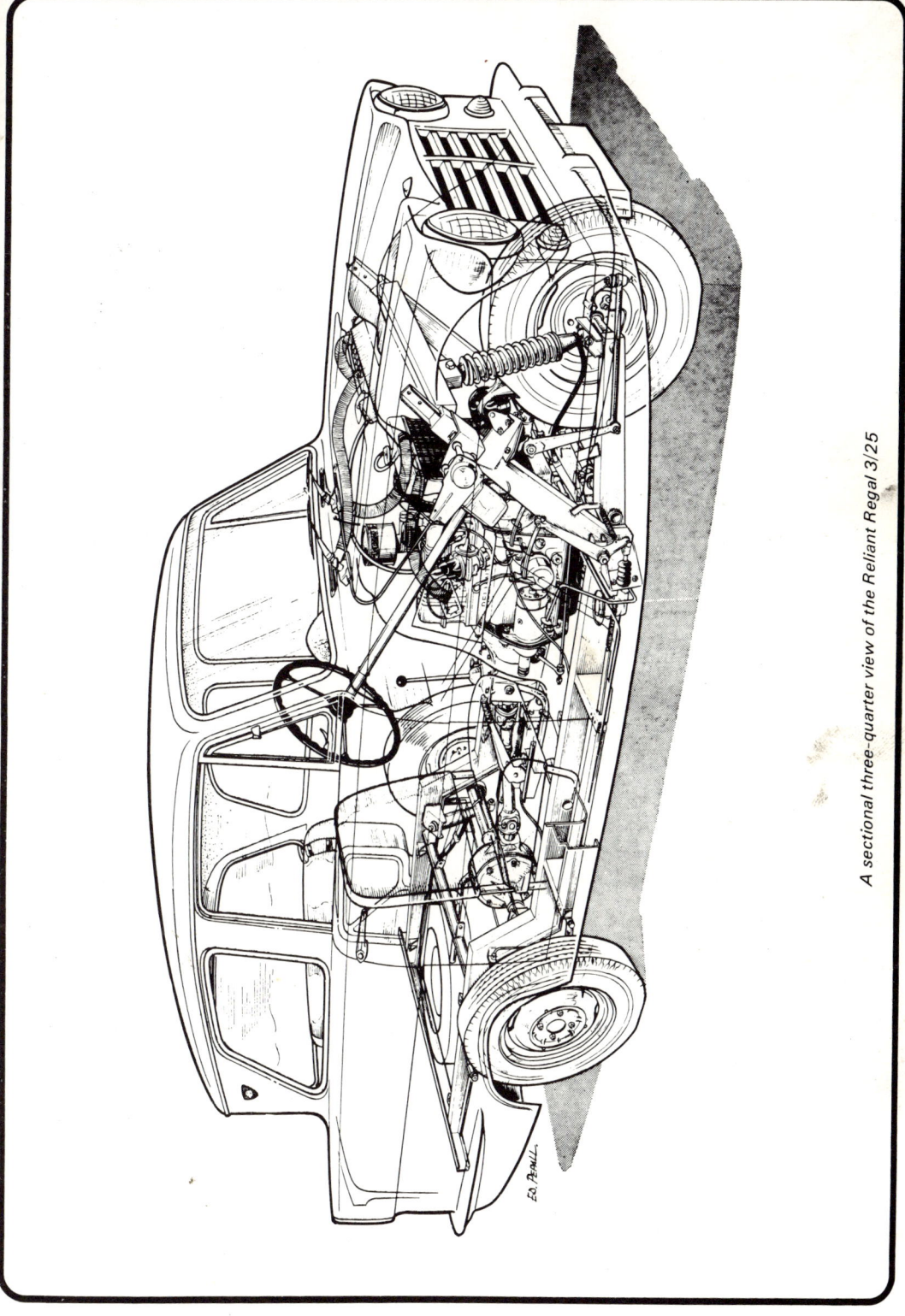

A sectional three-quarter view of the Reliant Regal 3/25

FUEL SYSTEM

Air cleaner

Regal models	gauze oil-soaked or renewable paper element type
Robin and Kitten models	renewable paper element type

Fuel pump
mechanical type

Carburettor

Regal models	Solex B28ZIC - 2 or Zenith 301Z
Kitten and Robin (848) models	SU HS2
Robin (748) models	Zenith 30 1Z or 30 1ZE
Fuel tank capacity (all models)	6.0 Imp gallons (27.2 litres)

Fuel octane rating
see *Filling Station Facts*

IGNITION SYSTEM

System type
coil and distributor with advance and retard mechanism

Distributor make and type

598 cc engine	Lucas 25 D4 (40872 A/D)
701 and early 748 cc engines	Lucas 41244A
Later 748 and all 848 cc engines	Lucas 43 D4

Distributor spindle rotation (viewed from top)

Lucas 25D4 type	clockwise
Lucas 41244A and 43D4 type	anti-clockwise

Contact breaker points gap

Lucas 41244A and D4 types	0.015 in (0.38 mm)
Lucas 43D4 type	0.016 - 0.018 in (0.40 - 0.45 mm)

Dwell angle

Lucas 41244A and 25D4 type	$60° \pm 3°$
Lucas 43D4 type	$51° \pm 5°$

Static ignition timing

Regal models	10° BTDC
Robin models (with 301Z carburettor)	TDC
Robin models (with 301ZE carburettor)	10° BTDC
Kitten models and Robin with SU carburettor	TDC

Spark plugs

Make and type:	
Regal models	Autolite AG 42, AC 44XLS or equivalent
Robin and Kitten models	Motorcraft AGR32
Electrode gap (all models)	0.025 in (0.64 mm)

STEERING AND SUSPENSION

Steering type

Regal and Robin models	worm and peg
Kitten model	rack and pinion

Steering geometry (Kitten)

Castor angle	12°
Camber angle	1° positive

King-pin inclination	9°
Toe-in	Parallel (Zero)

Suspension (Regal and Robin)

Front	patented leading arm type controlled by heavy duty coil spring and hydraulic damper unit
Rear	long semi-elliptical double leaf spring, rubber mounted with double-acting hydraulic damper units. Anti-roll bar (later Robin models only)

Suspension (Kitten)

Front	independent type with upper and lower wishbones with vertical links and assisted by coil springs and damper units
Rear	leaf springs, rubber mounted with double-acting damper units

Road wheels

Regal	pressed steel 13 x 3.5 in
Robin and Kitten	pressed steel 3.50B x 10 in or aluminium alloy 4.50 x 10 in

Tyres

Regal	Tubeless, 5.20 x 13 crossply
Robin:	
standard wheels	Tubeless, 5.20 x 10 crossply
optional wheels	Tubeless, 5.90 x 10 crossply
Kitten	145 x 10 radial ply

GEARBOX

Type	4 forward speeds and reverse (all models except Regal have synchromesh on all forward gears)

Ratios (Regal)

first	4.27 : 1
second	2.46 : 1
third	1.45 : 1
top	1.0 : 1
reverse	5.49 : 1

Ratios (Kitten and Robin)

first	3.88 : 1
second	2.05 : 1
third	1.32 : 1
top	1.0 : 1
reverse	3.25 : 1

Oil capacity (gearbox)

Regal models	1.0 Imp. pint (0.6 litres)
Robin and Kitten models	1.125 Imp. pint (0.64 litres)

CLUTCH (ALL MODELS)

Type	mechanical, single dry plate (Borg and Beck)
Diameter	6.25 in (159 mm)

VITAL STATISTICS

Actuation
    Regal models   Rod and lever
    Kitten and Robin models   cable linkage

Clearance
    Regal models $\frac{1}{2}$ in (12.7 mm) free movement at clutch pedal
    Kitten and Robin models $\frac{1}{16}$ in (1.5 mm) free movement of the clutch operating arm at the trunnion

REAR AXLE
Ratios
    Regal:
        Van   5.14 : 1
        Car   4.375 : 1
    Robin and Kitten   3.23 : 1

Oil capacity
    Regal models   2.0 Imp. pints (1.14 litres)
    Kitten and Robin models   2.25 Imp. pints (1.28 litres)

BRAKES
System type   hydraulically operated. internal expanding to all wheels, drums on all wheels

Drum diameter
    Front (all models except 701 cc Regal)   7 in (177.8 mm)
    Front Regal 701 cc models   8 in (203.2 mm)
    Rear (all models)   7 in (177.8 mm)

Adjustment   mechanical, at backplates

Handbrake   mechanical, acting on rear wheels

Fluid type   Castrol/Girling universal

ELECTRICAL SYSTEM
Type
    Regal 598 cc   12 volt, positive earth (ground)
    All other models   12 volt, negative earth (ground)

Starter motor   Lucas, inertia type

Generator
    Regal models   Lucas C40-1 dynamo with Lucas RB-106-2 regulator
    Kitten and Robin models   Lucas 15 ACR alternator

Lighting bulb chart (Regal models) — typical

	Voltage	Wattage	Cap type
Headlamps	12	60/45	Sealed beam
Pilot	12	5	Capless
Stop and tail	12	21/6	SBC Stagg
Front and rear flasher	12	21	SCC
Panel lights	12	2.2	MES
Warning light - oil	12	2.2	MES
Warning light - ignition	12	2.2	MES
Warning Light - main beam	12	2.2	MES
Flasher warning light	12	2.2	BA7S, MCC

Lighting bulb chart (Robin models) - typical

	Voltage	Wattage	Cap type
Headlamp - standard	12	60/45	Sealed beam
Headlamp - super models (quartz halogen)	12	60/55	Sealed beam
Headlamp - super models (quartz halogen)	12	60/55	Metal reflector
Pilot bulb	12	5	Capless
Stop and tail	12	21/5	SBC Stagg
Front and rear indicator	12	21	SCC
Main instrument illumination	12	3	Capless
Warning light - oil	12	3	Capless
Warning light - ignition	12	3	Capless
Warning light - main beam	12	3	Capless
Warning light - indicators	12	3	Capless
Warning light - rear screen switch	12	1.2	Capless
Warning light - hazard unit	12	2	BA7S
Interior lamp	12	6	Festoon
Battery indicator gauge illumination	12	2.2	MES
Oil pressure gauge illumination	12	2.2	MES
Number plate lamp	12	5	MCC

Lighting bulb chart (Kitten models) - typical

	Voltage	Wattage	Cap type
Headlamp	12	75/60	Sealed beam (rectangular)
Pilot bulb	12	5	Capless
Stop and tail	12	21/5	SBC Stagg
Front and rear indicator	12	21	SCC
Main instrument illumination	12	3	Capless
Warning light - oil	12	3	Capless
Warning light - ignition	12	3	Capless
Warning light - main beam	12	3	Capless
Warning light - indicators	12	3	Capless
Warning light - rear screen switch	12	1.2	Capless
Warning light - hazard unit	12	2	BA7S
Interior lamp	12	6	Festoon
Battery indicator gauge illumination	12	2.2	MES
Oil pressure gauge illumination	12	2.2	MES
Number plate lamp	12	5	MCC

Fuses (Regal models)

Fuse No and rating	Circuits protected
1 35 amp	accessories not controlled by ignition switch e.g. horns, lights etc.
2 35 amp	windscreen wipers, direction indicators, heater motor, fuel gauge and brake lights

Fuses (Robin & Kitten models)

Fuse position and rating	Circuits protected
Top 35 amp	battery circuit including headlamps, interior light and horn
2nd 35 amp	ignition controlled circuits including direction indicators, heater, wiper motor, instruments, gauges, hazard warning
3rd 35 amp	side lights, rear lights, number plate lamp, instrument panel illumination
4th 35 amp	'spare' on standard models — heated rear window where fitted

Separate in-line fuses are located behind the facia when auxiliary lamps or radio are fitted

41

DIMENSIONS, CAPACITIES, WEIGHTS

Dimensions – Regal

All models:	Inches	Mm
Wheelbase	76.0	1930.4
Track (rear)	46.0	1168.4
Ground clearance	6.0	152.4
Overall height	57.0	1447.8
Overall width	58.5	1505.9
Overall length	135.0	3429.0
Van only:		
Internal body length behind driver	48.0	1219.2
Internal body width	52.0	1295.4

Dimensions – Robin

	Saloon		Van	
	Inches	Mm	Inches	Mm
Overall length	131.0	3327.4	131.0	3327.4
Overall width	56.0	1422.4	56.0	1422.4
Overall height	54.0	1371.6	54.0	1371.6
Loading sill height	39.0	990.6	21.0	553.4
Load width (max.)	40.5	1028.7	33.5	850.9
Load height (max. aperture)	19.0	452.2	30.0	762.0
Interior load height (max.)	34.0	863.6	35.0	889.0
Length behind rear seat	23.0	584.2	26.5	693.1
Load length (rear seat folded)	42.5	1079.5	–	–
Length of load floor	–	–	49.0	1219.2
Load floor width	38.0	965.2	38.0	965.2

Dimensions – Kitten

	Saloon		Estate	
	Inches	Mm	Inches	Mm
Overall length	131.0	3327.4	131.75	3346.5
Overall width	56.0	1422.4	56.0	1422.4
Overall height	55.0	1397.0	55.0	1397.0
Loading sill height	40.0	1016.0	20.0	508.0
Load width (max.)	40.5	1028.7	33.5	850.9
Load height (max. aperture)	19.0	457.2	29.5	749.3
Interior load height (max.)	33.5	850.9	34.5	876.3
Length behind rear seat	25.5	647.7	26.5	693.1
Load length (rear seat folded)	43.0	1092.2	46.0	1168.4
Load floor width	37.5	952.5	37.5	952.5

Capacities – Robin

Saloon – capacity of boot area, rear seat up, spare wheel in position below tonneau cover	8.5 cu ft (0.231 cu m)
Saloon – capacity of rear compartment with rear seat folded, spare wheel in position, up to roof level	30.0 cu ft (0.849 cu m)
Van – total capacity of rear area, with spare wheel in position, including front passenger area	50.0 cu ft (1.416 cu m)
Van – capacity of complete rear compartment with spare wheel in position	40.0 cu ft (1.132 cu m)

Capacities – Kitten

Saloon – capacity of boot area, rear seat up, spare wheel in position below tonneau cover	8.5 cu ft (0.231 cu m)

Saloon – capacity of rear compartment with rear seat folded, spare wheel in position, up to roof level	30.0 cu ft (0.849 cu m)		
Estate – capacity of rear compartment, with spare wheel in position and rear seat up	9.5 cu ft (0.270 cu m)		
Estate – capacity of complete rear compartment, with spare wheel in position and rear seat folded	40.0 cu ft (1.132 cu m)		

Weights

Regal – unladen dry weight:

Saloon	884 lbs (401.34 kg)		
Van	885 lbs (401.79 kg)		

Robin (Saloon and Van):

Kerb weight	940 lbs (426.37 kg)		
Maximum payload (approx.)	770 lbs (349 kg)		

Kitten

	Saloon	*Estate*	*Van*
Kerb weight	1114 lbs (505.81 kg)	1187 lbs (538.90 kg)	1134 lbs 515.00 kg)
Maximum payload (approx.)	700 lbs (320 kg)	700 lbs (320 kg)	800 lbs (363 kg)

Tools for the Job

For anyone intending to tackle car servicing, a selection of good down-to-earth tools is a basic requirement. The initial outlay, even though it may appear to be something approaching the national defence budget, could well be less than the labour charges for one full service; on top of this, you should be paying less for the oil and replacement parts by getting them yourself so, provided you've two or three hours to spare, you must be on to a winner.

A small but important point when buying tools is the quality. You don't have to buy the very best in the shop but, on the other hand, the cheapest probably aren't much good. Have a word with the manager or proprietor if you're in doubt, he'll tell you what's good value for money.

It's very difficult to tell you exactly what you're going to need, but the list below should be a great help in building up a good tool kit. Combination spanners (ring one end, open-ended the other) are recommended because, although more expensive than double open-ended ones, they give the advantages of both types).

Combination spanners to cover the range $\frac{1}{4}$ to 1 in AF
Adjustable spanner – 9 inch
Spark plug spanner (with rubber insert)
Spark plug gap adjustment tool
Set of feeler gauges
Brake adjuster spanner ($\frac{1}{4}$ in AF, square)
Screwdriver – 4 in blade x $\frac{1}{4}$ in dia (plain)
Screwdriver – 4 in blade x $\frac{1}{4}$ in dia (crosshead)
Pliers – 6 inch
Junior hacksaw
Tyre pump

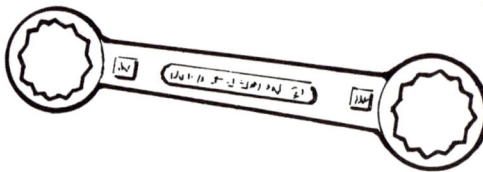

Double ended ring spanner

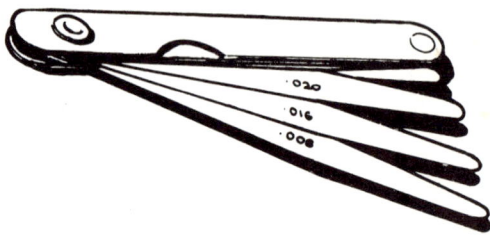

Feeler gauges

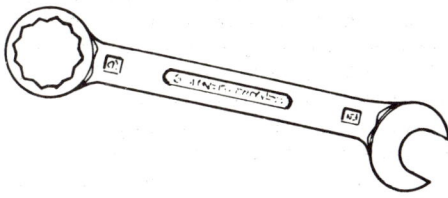

Combination ring/flat spanner

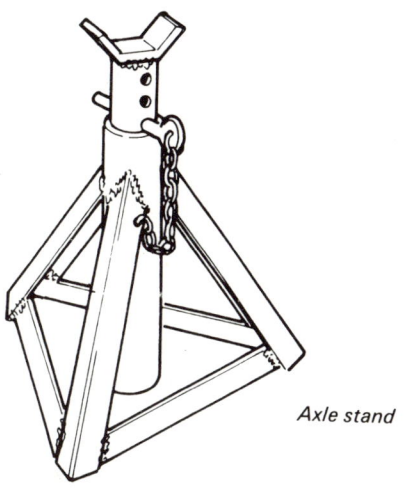

Axle stand

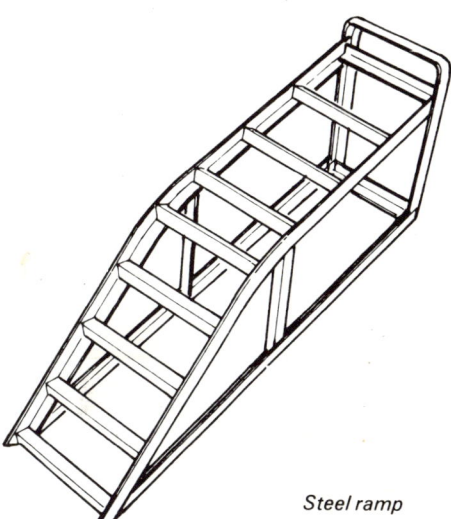

Steel ramp

Tyre pressure gauge
Grease gun
Oil can
Fine emery cloth or oilstone
Wire brush (small)
Funnel (medium size)
Hydraulic jack or strong scissor type
Pair of axle stands (concrete or wooden blocks
will do if you're careful about choosing them)
Hose brush

You may find that a pair of metal ramps is a very useful investment, providing an alternative to the jack or axle stands when you want to get at the underside of the car but don't need to remove the wheel(s). Most ramps available give a lift of between 9 inches and 1 ft and you can, of course, drive either the front or back end of the car on to them – but you'll still need to apply the handbrake and chock the other wheel(s) for safety's sake.

Hopefully, your attempts at car servicing are going to show you that it can all be worthwhile, and having worked your way through the various jobs listed in the Service Schedules you'll be able to see that there are many others which can be done without becoming a mechanical wizard. For this purpose, Haynes publish a first class Owner's Workshop Manuals for the Regal, Robin and Kitten which detail just about every operation that can conceivably be done on these cars. It'll mean buying a few more tools, but you'll save yourself still more money and get a good job done in the process.

While we're talking about tools, it's worth mentioning some of the tune-up aids that are on the market. A visit to a good motor accessory shop can be an enlightening experience, just to show you the sort of things available. Later in this book, you'll find a bit about 'bolt-on goodies', but all we'll concern ourselves with here are three items.

Stroboscopic timing light

The most accurate way of checking ignition timing (that's the time at which the spark occurs) is with the engine running, and for this a stroboscopic (strobe) light is used. This is connected to No. 1 spark plug lead and the beam is shone on to the crankshaft pulley mark. Any proprietary light is supplied with full connecting and operating instructions.

Dwell angle meter

This is used for measuring the period of time for which the distributor points remain closed during the ignition cycle of one cylinder, and provides a more accurate method of setting-up the ignition than can be done by simply setting the points gap. Dwell angle meters normally incorporate a tachometer (rev **45** counter if you prefer), which can be useful for checking engine idle speed.

Cylinder compression gauge

This is very useful for tracing the cause of a fall-off in engine performance. It consists of a pressure gauge and non-return valve, and is simply screwed into a spark plug hole while the engine is turned over on the starter.

Two other useful items are a hydrometer, which is used for checking the specific gravity of the battery electrolyte (this will tell you if you have a dud cell which won't hold a charge), and a 12-volt lamp on an extension lead with crocodile clips which can be connected to the battery terminals.

Care of your tools

Having bought a reasonable set of tools and equipment, it's the easiest thing in the world to abuse them. After use, always wipe off any dirt and grease using a clean, dry cloth before putting them away. Never leave them lying around after they've been used. A simple rack on the garage wall, for things you don't need to carry in the car, is a good idea.

Keep all your spanners and the like in a metal box — you can wrap some rags around them to stop them rattling if you're going to carry them in the boot of the car. Any gauges and meters should be carefully put away so that they don't get damaged or rusty. Do take a little care over maintaining your tools too. Screwdriver blades, for example, inevitably lose their keen edges, and a little timely attention with a file won't go amiss.

Service Scene

We've now discussed some of the more important features of the cars, and some equally important points about tools, money saving and so on. Now to the nitty gritty of servicing – perhaps the very thing that you've dreaded for so long...? The Reliant Regal, Robin and Kitten models are a pretty basic design, which means that they're built in a traditional manner (engine at the front, gearbox behind it and the drive transmitted through the rear axle); so they're simple in concept and easy to work on.

But don't be misled into thinking that Reliant are just old-fashioned in their engineering. By sticking to traditional designs and layouts they know that the component parts will be reliable and have an extended life. 'Good', you might think, 'I won't have to bother with servicing and maintenance because the parts will last for ever'. Let's understand right from the start that it's still important to carry out servicing and inspections at regular intervals in the interests of safety and reliability.

The old maxim of 'prevention is better than cure' could never be more appropriately applied than in connection with car servicing. Whether it be casting an observant eye over the general workings of the car or setting about the service tasks in a workmanlike (or workwomanlike) fashion, it's all going to be worthwhile in the long run. Remember always that a worn part won't put itself right and isn't a thing to be lived with. Fix it as soon you find it, even if it's not time for the next service.

We've tried to present the servicing tasks that follow in a logical way to minimize the amount of jacking up, etc which may be a prelude to the actual job. The items listed are basically those recommended by Reliant, but are supplemented by

some additional ones which we think are well worth the extra time and trouble.

Safety

Accidents do happen but the vast majority could be prevented by taking a little care. In the list below we've put together a list of points which, if observed, could greatly reduce your chances of having an accident when working on your car. You may think that some are obvious, but how many times have you forgotten to observe some elementary precautions? The list below is an attempt to make you 'safety conscious' then hopefully you'll live to enjoy the fruits of your labours!

DON'T run the engine in the garage with the doors closed – exhaust fumes are highly poisonous.

DON'T work in an inspection pit with the engine running – the fumes will tend to concentrate at the lowest point.

DO keep long hair, sleeves, ties and the like well clear of any rotating parts when the engine's running.

DON'T grab hold of ignition HT leads when the engine's running – there's just the possibility of an electric shock, particularly if the leads are dirty and wet.

47

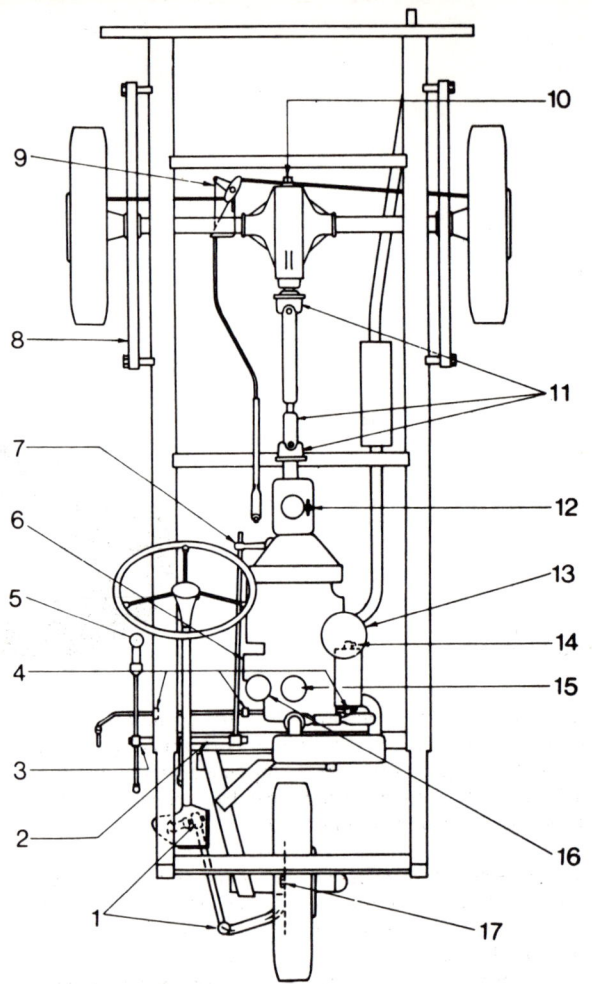

Lubrication Chart – early Regal models

1	Track rod (2 fittings)	Multi-purpose grease
2	Clutch crossshaft (1 fitting)	Multi-purpose grease
3	Brake lever pivot (1 point)	Engine oil
4	Accelerator cross-shaft (3 points)	Engine oil
5	Brake master cylinder reservoir	Hydraulic brake and clutch fluid (SAE J1703)
6	Engine oil filter	–
7	Clutch operating rod (1 point)	Engine oil
8	Spring leaves	Penetrating oil
9	Brake rod compensator	Multi-purpose grease
10	Rear axle	Hypoid gear oil (SAE 90 EP)
11	Propeller shaft (3 fittings)	Multi-purpose grease
12	Gearbox	10W/40 engine oil
13	Air cleaner	Engine oil (for oil wetted type)
14	Dynamo	Engine oil
15	Engine	Multigrade engine oil, SAE 20W/50
16	Distributor	Engine oil and petroleum jelly
17	Stub axle (2 fittings)	Multi-purpose grease

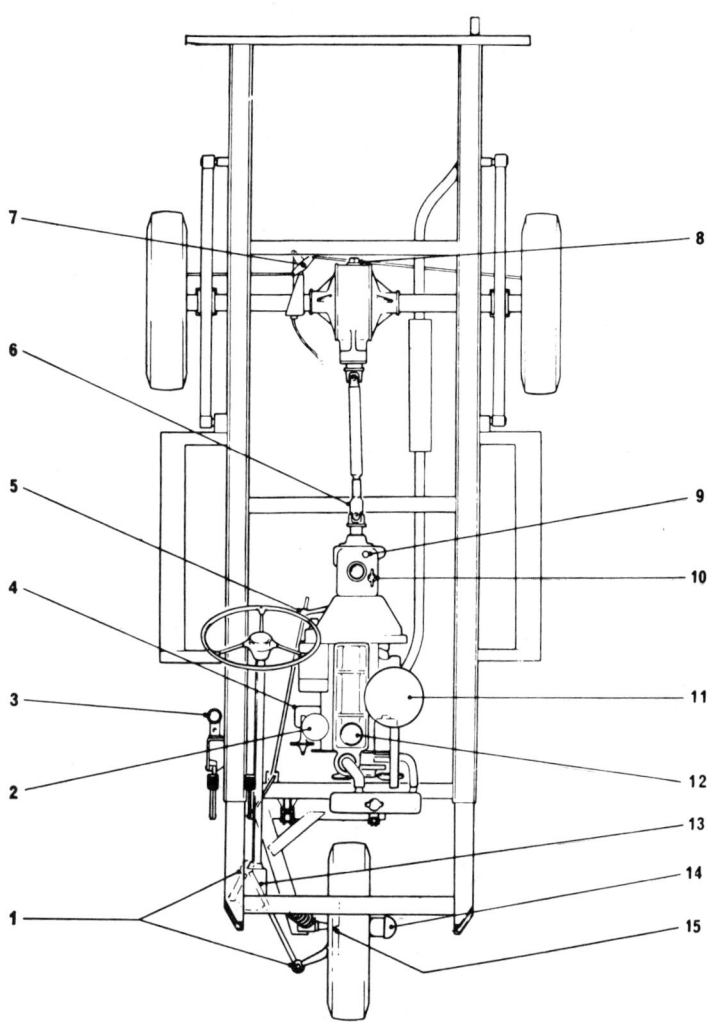

Lubrication Chart – Regal de Luxe, Super and 3/30

1	Track rod (2 grease nipples)	Multi-purpose grease
2	Distributor	Engine oil and petroleum jelly
3	Brake master cylinder reservoir	Hydraulic brake and clutch fluid (SAE J 1703)
4	Engine oil filter	—
5	Clutch operating arm	Lithium based grease
6	Propeller shaft (3 nipples)	Multi-purpose grease
7	Brake rod compensator (2 nipples)	Multi-purpose grease
8	Rear axle	Hypoid gear oil, SAE 90 EP
9	Gearbox	Hypoid gear oil, SAE 80 EP
10	Gearbox dipstick	—
11	Air cleaner	Engine oil (for oil-wetted type only)
12	Engine	Multigrade engine oil, SAE 20W/50
13	Steering box	Hypoid gear oil, SAE 80 EP
14	Front hub	Lithium based grease
15	Swivel pin (2 nipples)	Multi-purpose grease

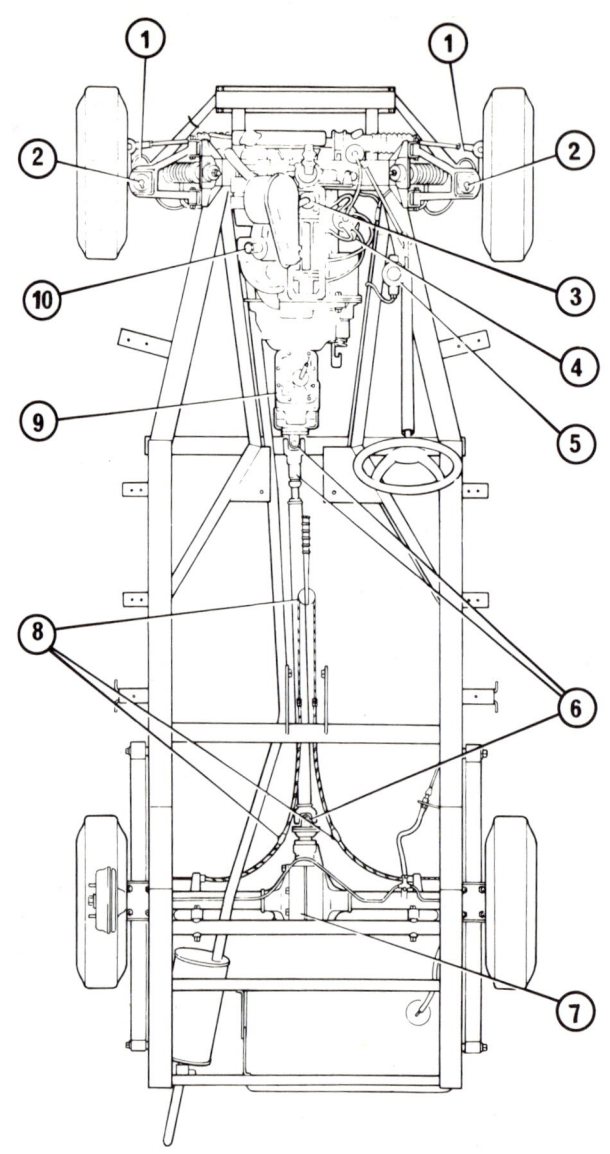

Lubrication chart – Kitten models

1	Lower trunnion (2 nipples)	Multi-purpose grease
2	Upper ball joint (2 nipples)	Multi-purpose grease
3	Engine	Multigrade engine oil, SAE 20W/50
4	Engine oil filter	–
5	Brake master cylinder	Hydraulic brake and clutch fluid (SAE J 1703)
6	Propeller shaft (3 nipples)	Multi-purpose grease
7	Rear axle	Hypoid gear oil, SAE 90 EP
8	Handbrake cable (2 nipples)	Multi-purpose grease
9	Gearbox	Multi-purpose grease
10	Carburettor dashpot	Hypoid gear oil, SAE 80 EP

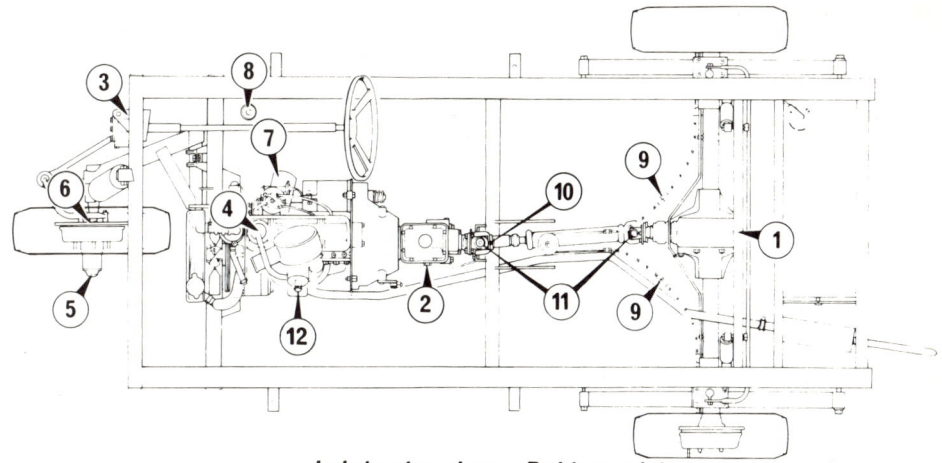

Lubrication chart – Robin models

1	Rear axle	*Hypoid gear oil, SAE 90 EP*
2	Gearbox	*Hypoid gear oil, SAE 80 EP*
3	Steering box	*Hypoid gear oil, SAE 80 EP*
4	Engine	*Multigrade engine oil, SAE 20W/50*
5	Front hub	*Lithium based grease*
6	Front swivel pin (2 nipples)	*Multi-purpose grease*
7	Engine oil filter	*–*
8	Master cylinder	*Hydraulic brake and clutch fluid (SAE J1703)*
9	Handbrake cable (2 nipples)	*Multi-purpose grease*
10	Propeller shaft sliding joint (1 nipple)	*Multi-purpose grease*
11	Propeller shaft universal joints (2 nipples) ...	*Multi-purpose grease*
12	Carburettor dashpot (models with SU carburettor)	*Engine oil*

DO check the rear wheels when jacking up the front of the car, and vice versa. Where possible, also apply the handbrake and engage first or reverse gear.

DON'T rely on the car jack when you're working underneath. Axle stands, or wooden or concrete blocks should be used, placed under the rear or front chassis frames.

DO wipe up oil or grease from the floor if you spill any (and you will do, sooner or later).

DO get someone to check regularly that everything's OK if you're likely to be spending some time underneath the car.

DON'T use a file or similar tool without a handle. The tang can give you a nasty gash if something goes wrong.

DO make sure when you're using a spanner that it's the right size for the nut and that it's properly fitted before tightening or loosening.

DO brush away any drilling swarf with an old paintbrush – never your fingers.

DON'T allow battery acid or battery terminal corrosion to contact the skin or clothes. If it should happen, wash off immediately with plenty of cold running water.

DON'T rush any job – that's how mistakes are made. If you don't think you'll finish the job in time, do it tomorrow, but try not to make this an excuse for forgetting about it.

DO take care when pouring out brake fluid. If it spills on the paintwork and isn't removed immediately, it'll take the paint off. And wash your hands well afterwards as it's poisonous.

SERVICE SCHEDULES

WEEKLY, BEFORE A LONG JOURNEY, OR EVERY 250 MILES

The following tools, lubricants etc., are likely to be needed:

Tyre pressure gauge, wheel nut spanner, lint free cloth, tyre tread depth gauge.

Multigrade engine oil, distilled water, clean tap water, windscreen washer detergent sachet (anti-freeze type in winter), antifreeze.

1 Check engine oil level (car on level ground)

The engine oil dipstick's on the left-hand side of **51**

the engine, next to the generator. If the engine has just been running, wait a minute or two for the oil to drain back to the sump, then pull the dipstick up and out. Wipe it clean on a lint-free cloth, then put it back in to its full depth; now pull it out again and check the level. Add oil if necessary, to bring it up to the 'Full' mark on the dipstick — don't overfill because it's not only wasteful but can also find its way out of the engine by overloading gaskets and oil seals.

Take care when pouring in the oil (the filler's on the forward end of the rocker cover), and allow it to drain into the sump before rechecking the level. When you're satisfied that the job's completed, ensure that the dipstick and filler cap are properly fitted, then wipe away any spilt oil from the rocker cover.

2 Check battery electrolyte level

First wipe away any dirt or moisture from the top of the battery so that none can get inside. Remove the caps or cover from the battery cells, and check the electrolyte level. Add distilled water to bring the level just above the tops of the battery plates.

If for some reason you've got no distilled water (and it does happen) you can use the frost which collects on the walls of your freezer or fridge, and allow this to melt; if you're really desperate, and as a last resort only, boil up some water in a kettle then allow it to cool, but don't make a habit of it or the battery will suffer in the long run. Refit the cell caps or battery cover, carefully wiping up any drops of water that were spilt, then check that the terminals are tight.

A very light smear of petroleum jelly (Vaseline) can be applied to help prevent any corrosion from getting a foothold. If the weather's extremely cold, run the engine for a few minutes; this will charge the battery and mix the electrolyte which will prevent the added water from freezing.

3 Check brake master cylinder reservoir level

The brake fluid reservoir's located under the floor of the driver's footwell (Regal models) or in the engine compartment above the driver's footwell (Robin and Kitten models). Before unscrewing the reservoir cap, wipe away any dirt with a clean, dry cloth to prevent any falling into the reservoir when the cap's removed. Top up the reservoir if necessary with Castrol Girling Universal brake fluid.

If there's a marked drop in the level when you check it, there's a leakage somewhere which must be traced and rectified urgently. If you can't find the source of the leakage then get your Reliant dealer to carry out an inspection immediately.

Don't forget to wipe up any fluid spillage — it won't do the bodywork any good if left on it. Refit the reservoir cap after you've checked that the vent hole is clear.

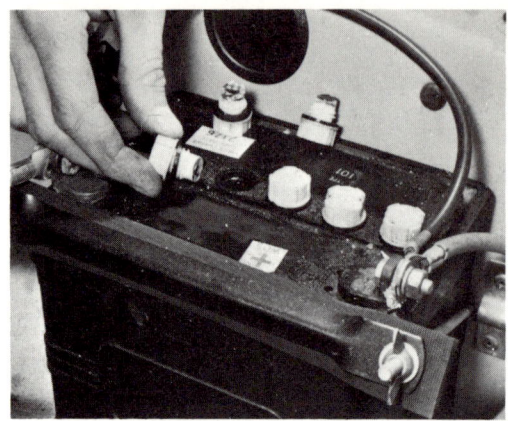

Checking the battery electrolyte level

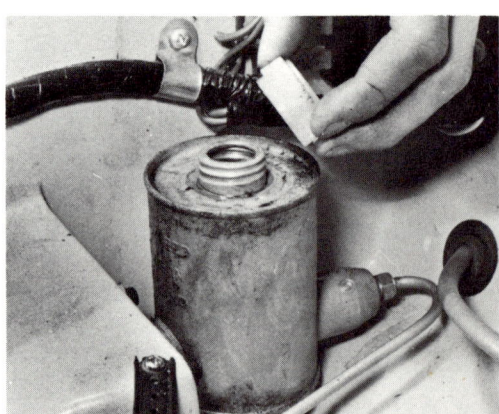

Checking the brake master cylinder fluid level (Kitten model shown)

Location of brake master cylinder reservoir (Regal models)

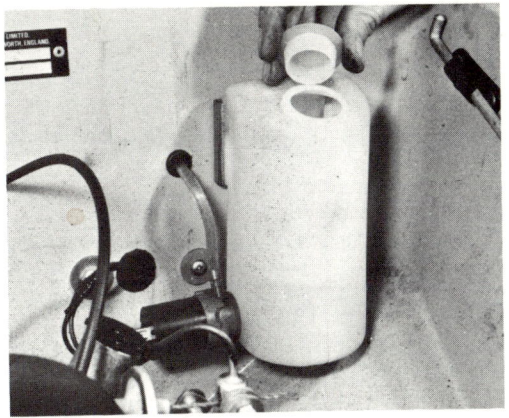

Checking the windscreen washer reservoir level (Kitten model shown)

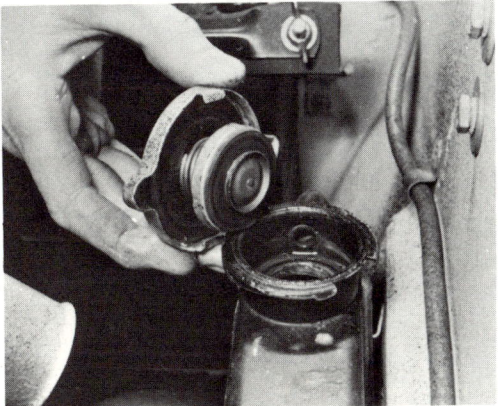

Checking the radiator coolant level

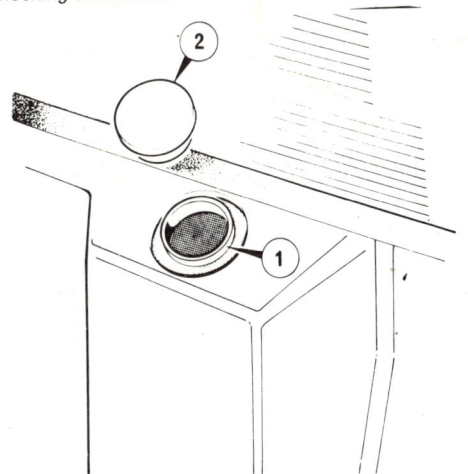

The rear screen washer reservoir located in the rear door (Kitten estate model)

4   Top up windscreen washer reservoir

Add water as necessary to the windscreen washer reservoir, together with a little of one of the proprietary detergent products for windscreens. In winter, use an antifreeze type (but NOT cooling system antifreeze). Where a rear screen washer is fitted (Kitten estate models) the reservoir is fitted in the rear door as shown in the illustration.

5   Check engine coolant level

Never remove the radiator pressure cap if the engine's hot; if you do, boiling water may shoot everywhere and you could get severely burnt. If the system's warm, remove the cap, slowly turning it anti-clockwise to let the pressure escape, then remove it and top up.

Some Robin and Kitten models have a radiator that has a coolant level indicator visible in the filler neck. The correct level for other Robin and Kitten models is when the top header tank of the radiator is two-thirds full. On Regal models, it's necessary to ensure that the coolant level is just up to the bottom of the filler neck.

If topping up the radiator becomes a regular task, you're obviously losing some coolant, which spells danger. Causes of loss may be loose or perished hoses, a faulty seal on the radiator cap, a leaking radiator or heater, or a blown cylinder head gasket. If you can't find the fault, get it looked into straight away by the local Reliant dealer before your troubles really start.

If only a very small quantity of coolant is required you can get away with adding water only, but remember you're diluting the antifreeze strength, so beware, especially in winter. Preferably top up with an antifreeze/water mixture as generally used in the system — for further information on this, see the 24 000 miles Service Schedules, later on.

When you've topped up the system, ensure that the cap seal's clean, then refit the cap.

6   Check tyre pressures and tread condition

With the tyres cold, check their pressures (see *Filling Station Facts*). If possible, use your own gauge — those on garage forecourts tend to be abused and inaccurate. Don't forget the spare wheel; the pressure here should be up to the maximum ever likely to be needed, then it can be adjusted if necessary when the wheel is used.

With the tyres properly inflated, run your hands and eyes over the tyre walls and tread. This is best done with the wheel off the ground so that it can be rotated but, if you're really not feeling up to it, move the car along backwards or forwards a foot or so, so that you can check all round. The tread depth must not be less than 1 mm throughout at least three- **53** quarters of the width, and around its full circumference.

You can buy gauges for checking this, but a 2p piece inserted in the tread groove can be used. If the tread's not deeper than the distance from the row of dots to the edge of the coin, you're breaking the law, so get some replacements pretty quickly. There must also be no cuts, bulges or other deformities; if these are present, you're also breaking the law.

If you've got to buy new tyres, read the bit in *Save It!*, but remember that it's illegal to fit a radial and a crossply tyre on the same axle, and that radials may not be fitted on the front if you've got crossplies on the back. In the case of Regal and Robin models Reliant recommend that only crossply tyres are fitted.

7 Check tightness of wheel nuts

While you're down at floor level, it's a good time to check the tightness of the wheel nuts. Where hub caps are fitted remove them (if you've got to use a screwdriver, take care with the chrome and paintwork). Now just check that the nuts are tight using the spanner supplied for the job. There's no need to stand on the spanner because someday the wheel will have to come off, but the nuts should be tightened firmly. Don't forget to refit the hub cap (where applicable) afterwards.

8 Check that all the lights work

Switch on the car lights and check that everything works correctly. If any bulbs need renewing, refer to *In an Emergency* where the procedures are given. Don't forget to include the brake lights and indicators in this check, and finally see that the lamp lenses are clean, front and rear.

EVERY 3000 MILES OR 3 MONTHS, WHICHEVER COMES FIRST

(in addition to the items listed in the Weekly/250 miles Schedule)

The following tools, lubricants etc are likely to be needed:

Sump drain plug spanner, grease gun, oil can, miscellaneous spanners, hydrometer (if available).

Multigrade engine oil, windscreen wiper blades, Vaseline.

1 Change engine oil

Note: The engine oil is normally changed at intervals of 6000 miles or 6 months, but under certain adverse conditions more frequent changing is required. Such conditions include repeated stop/start driving (where the choke is frequently being used), driving in extremely cold or extremely hot conditions, where it is very dusty. The procedure for oil changing is given in the 6000 mile Schedule, together with renewal of the filter.

2 Check fan belt tension

The 'V' sectioned drive belt from the engine crankshaft pulley not only drives the fan (as its name suggests) but also the water pump which is behind the fan pulley and the generator (dynamo or alternator). Failure of this rather insignificant item has ruined many a journey, and it must be inspected regularly. When checking the belt not only are you looking for slackness, but also for any signs of fraying of the belt fabric and splitting of the rubber compound.

A slack or damaged fan belt not only affects cooling and charging, but can produce some pretty awful shrieking and rumbling noises on occasions.

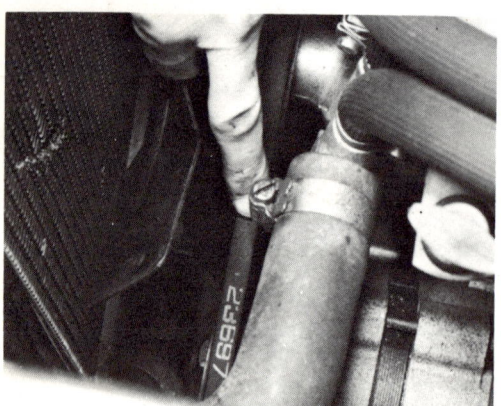

Checking the fan belt tension

The generator adjuster link bracket

The correct tension's given in *Vital Statistics* and if your belt's in need of adjustment here's how to do it.

Loosen the two pivot bolts which attach the generator to the engine. Now loosen the adjusting link nuts and bolts (at each end) and pull the generator away from the engine. A bit of leverage can be used, but with an alternator this must be at the drive end bracket only or you'll damage it. Tighten all the nuts and bolts when the tension's correct.

If the belt's to be removed, loosen the generator mounting and adjustment bolts as already described, and peel the belt off the pulleys. After fitting a new belt, the tension should be rechecked after about 250 miles of running, because new belts tend to stretch a little in use.

3 Check and clean battery

If you've got a hydrometer, now's the time to use it to check your battery specific gravity (SG for short). Assuming that it's fully charged, the SG should be as given in the table below according to the battery temperature. If the battery's been on charge recently, leave it for an hour or two if you can, as it warms up when being charged.

If one cell has a low reading it indicates loss of electrolyte (unlikely unless the casing's cracked) or an internal fault. In either case, your battery will soon require renewing – so be prepared to replace it before it lets you down.

Battery fully charged	
SG	Electrolyte temperature
1.268	100° F or 38° C
1.272	90° F or 32° C
1.276	80° F or 27° C
1.280	70° F or 21° C
1.284	60° F or 16° C
1.288	50° F or 10° C
1.292	40° F or 4° C
1.286	30° F or -1.5° C

Battery fully discharged	
SG	Electrolyte temperature
1.098	100° F or 38° C
1.102	90° F or 32° C
1.106	80° F or 27° C
1.110	70° F or 21° C
1.114	60° F or 16° C
1.118	50° F or 10° C
1.122	40° F or 4° C
1.126	30° F or -1.5° C

From time to time corrosion may appear on the battery terminals or on the ends of the main battery leads. Where this has occurred, detach the leads, release the clamp and lift out the battery. A solution of warm water and bicarbonate of soda will remove all the corrosion; brush it on to the terminals, making

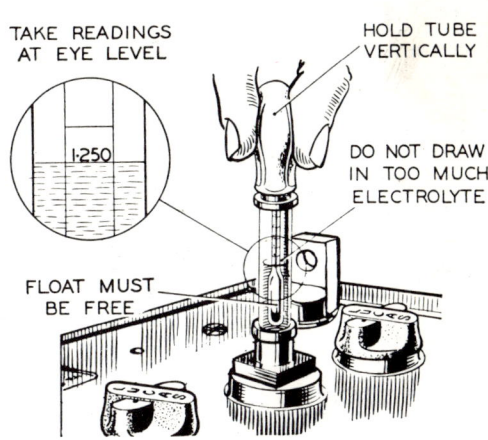

Using a hydrometer to check the battery Specific Gravity (SG)

sure that none gets inside. Dip the lead ends straight into the mixture, but too much corrosion will neutralise it so you may need a second mix. Clean the metal clamp bracket assembly in the same way.

During all this, take care that the mixture doesn't get into your eyes, as there's a certain amount of splashing and bubbling as it does its work. When everything's clean again wipe every part dry with a clean cloth. Smear the clamp plate assembly with Vaseline before refitting and clamping the battery in position. Reconnect the leads and smear a little more Vaseline on the lead ends and terminals.

4 Check brake adjustment, brake pedal travel and handbrake operation

The brake pedal travel and handbrake lever travel are automatically adjusted with the rear brakes. It's only after a very high mileage that you're ever likely to find that the handbrake cables have stretched and need adjustment, but if it is necessary the procedure's quite straightforward.

Rear brakes: To adjust the rear brakes, raise the rear of the car, but don't forget to release the handbrake and chock the front wheel(s). It's a good idea to place axle stands or strong packing blocks in position just in case the jack should fail. Lubricate the brake adjusters, and then turn each adjuster in a clockwise direction (looking at the backplate) until the roadwheel can't be turned by hand; the brake shoes will then be locked against the brake drum. Now slacken each adjuster until the wheels will just rotate freely, and the job's done.

Handbrake: Now apply the handbrake until it's on the third notch of the ratchet. If the handbrake's adjusted correctly it should just be possible to rotate the rear wheels, an equal amount of force being

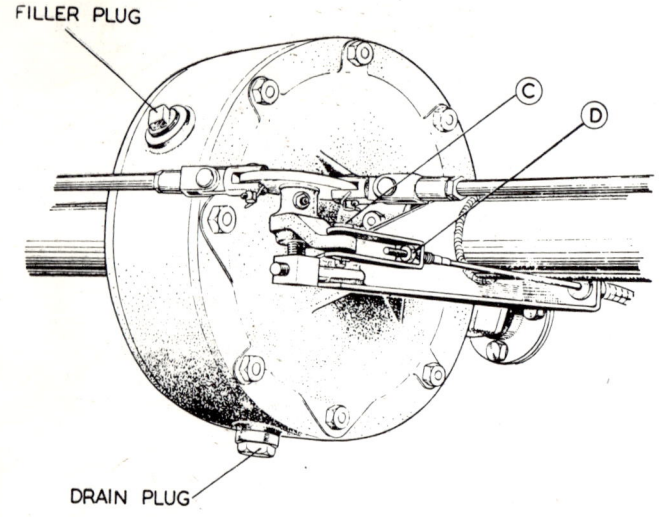

FILLER PLUG

DRAIN PLUG

The handbrake cable adjustment point (Regal models)
C Rear brake balance lever assembly
D Handbrake adjuster

required for each wheel. If you find that adjustment is needed, this is done as follows:

Regal models – Turn each rear wheel brake adjuster until the brake shoes are locked against the drums (the handbrake lever must be in the 'off' position during this adjustment). Remove the split pin from the clevis pin at the point where the handbrake cable joins the balance lever at the rear of the car. The cable can now be adjusted by slackening the locknut at the forward end of the handbrake cable clevis and screwing up the other nut to the clevis, thus effectively reducing the length of the handbrake cable.

When the handbrake cable's correctly adjusted, the clevis pin will slide easily into the clevis and balance lever without any undue strain being placed on any component. Finally tighten the clevis lock/adjuster nuts and fit a new split pin to the clevis pin. The brake adjusters can now be backed off until the road wheels rotate freely.

Robin and Kitten models – Having adjusted the rear brakes as described previously, apply the handbrake lever until its on the third notch of the ratchet. Slacken the cable locknuts and turn each of the cable adjusters to take up any slackness in the cables. Check that the cables aren't over-adjusted by turning each of the rear wheels in turn. Finally retighten the cable locknuts and that's the job done.

Front brakes: To adjust the front brakes is an almost identical job to the rear brake adjustment except that each brake shoe has its own adjuster. Apply the handbrake, chock the rear wheels, raise the front of the car and support it. Lubricate the adjusters and turn one of the adjusters in an anti-clockwise direction to bring its friction lining away from the drum.

Turn the second adjuster clockwise until the wheel's locked, then turn the adjuster anti-clockwise until the wheel can be rotated by hand without binding. Repeat the locking and unlocking procedure with the first adjuster.

5 Lubricate all hinges, locks and catches

Apply a drop or two of oil to all the moving and contact points of the door hinges and locks, bonnet hinges, lock and safety catch, and boot or tailgate hinges and lock. Wipe off any surplus, as it collects dirt and will mark the paintwork or someone's clothes if it's left to run. Lubricate the lock barrels by applying a little oil to the key and inserting it two or three times. Wipe the key and lock barrel afterwards to remove any surplus.

Apply a trace of general purpose grease to the lock contact points of the striker plates. Again, wipe off the surplus before it gets on to clothing.

6 Lubricate carburettor controls

Apply a drop or two of oil to the control linkage and pivot points of the carburettor. There are several different types of carburettor set-up, so you'll need to check exactly what you've got on your car but, if it moves, lubricate it! Also apply a drop to the accelerator pedal pivot.

Most Robin and all Kitten models are fitted with an SU carburettor and the dashpot oil level should be checked periodically. To do this, unscrew the black hexagon plug from the top of the carburettor suction chamber and withdraw the damper. Top up the dashpot until the oil level is $\frac{1}{2}$ in (13 mm) above the top of the hollow piston rod. Use an SAE 20 or 20/50 grade engine oil to top up the dashpot, then refit the damper and screw down the hexagon plug.

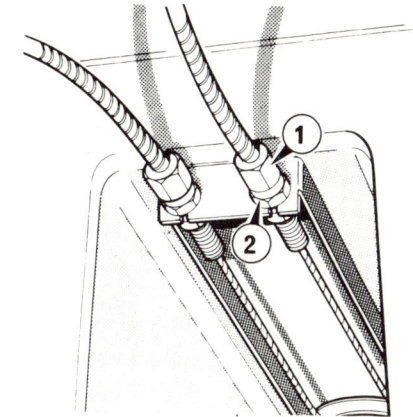

Handbrake cable adjustment points (Robin and Kitten models)

1   Adjuster nut   2   Locknut

Lubricate handbrake clevis (arrowed) - (Robin and Kitten models)

Apply a little grease to the handbrake cable guides (Robin and Kitten models)

Grease the balance lever and fulcrum and lubricate the clevis (Regal models)

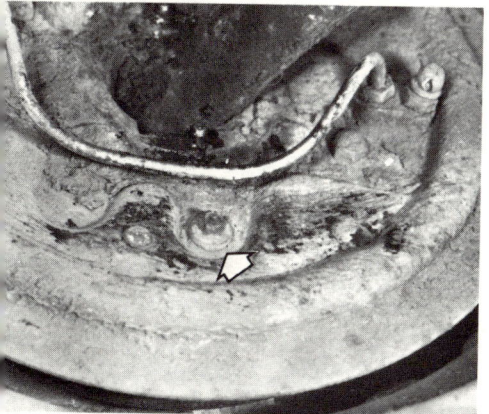

Location of the lower front brake adjuster (Regal model shown)

Using a brake adjuster spanner to adjust the rear brake (Kitten model shown). Roadwheel removed for clarity

EVERY 6000 MILES OR 6 MONTHS, WHICHEVER COMES FIRST

(in addition to the items listed in the Weekly and 3000-mile Schedules)

The following tools, lubricants etc are likely to be needed:

Sump drain plug spanner, oil can, feeler gauges, stroboscopic timing light (if available), spark plug spanner, tachometer (if available), miscellaneous spanners and screwdrivers, grease gun.

Multigrade engine oil, gearbox, rear axle, and steering gear oil, contact breaker set, rocker cover gasket, oil filter element, air cleaner element, set of relined brake shoes.

1 Change engine oil and filter

Oil changes should be made only when the engine is warm, as this allows the oil to drain out more quickly. So if it's not warm, drive around for a mile or two – this is better than leaving a cold engine idling because less wear takes place.

Now get a suitable container handy which will fit beneath the sump. It's got to be fairly shallow, and at the same time be able to hold about 6 pints (3.5 litres) – and old plastic washing-up bowl is the sort of thing that will do the job. Alternatively you could use an old gallon oil can, laid on its side with a square cut out of it to catch the oil (but don't forget to screw the cap on!).

Now get ready for the dirty part and roll up your sleeves. Lie on the ground and remove the sump drain plug. You're bound to get a little oil on your fingers, and possibly all over your hand, so do it as quickly as possible. If you should drop the drain plug in the container, don't forget it's there – you're going to need it later on.

The draining operation will take about 15 minutes so you can now think about the filter. You'll need another small container to catch the oil in the filter, but if you're quick enough in removing it you won't spill much. Grasp the filter assembly with both hands and unscrew it (in an anti-clockwise direction). Discard the filter and wipe away any oil from the filter mating face on the cylinder block.

Lubricate sparingly, with clean engine oil, the rubber sealing ring attached to the new filter before screwing it into position. Don't overtighten the filter as the screw threads can easily be stripped, and besides you'll have great difficulty in removing it next time.

Now wipe around the sump drain plug hole, check that the sealing washer's undamaged, and refit the plug. Wipe away any oil with a rag. The new engine oil can now be added to bring the level up to the 'Full' mark on the dipstick. Start the engine and run it at a fast idle for about a minute. Stop the engine

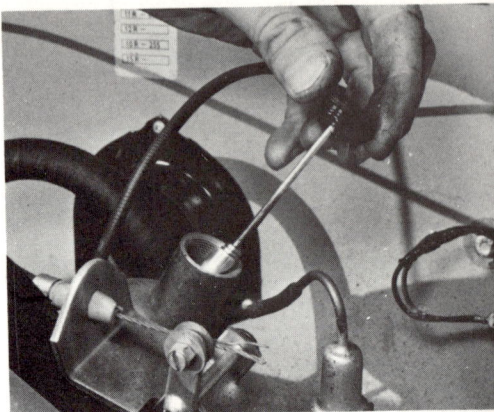

Removing the carburettor damper to check the dashpot oil level (Robin and Kitten models with SU carburettor)

The sump drain plug (arrowed)

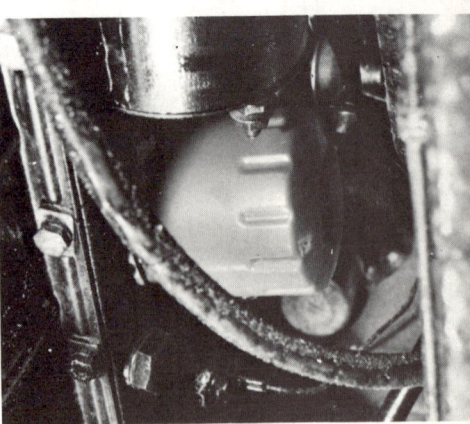

The engine oil filter unit

Topping up the engine oil (Kitten model shown)

Removing a sparking plug using the correct size socket spanner

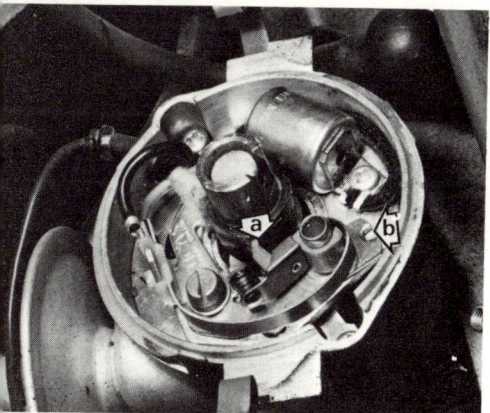

The Lucas 45D4 distributor, with cap and rotor removed, as fitted to Robin and Kitten models. A-heel of moving contact on top of the cam. B-point at which to insert screwdriver when moving the fixed contact during adjustments

again and wait a few minutes before checking the oil level once more. Add oil as necessary to bring it back up to the 'Full' mark on the dipstick. Now just check that there aren't any signs of leakage from the oil filter or sump drain plug.

There's always a problem with disposing of old oil, but if you buy it in 5 litre cans you can put the old oil in there and let the dustman take it away. You can't just tip it down your household drain as that's illegal, but some garages will take it off your hands if they've got disposal arrangements with a recycling firm.

2   Service air filter assembly

Note: The air cleaner element's normally renewed at intervals of 12 000 miles or 12 months, but under very dusty conditions it's advisable to renew it more frequently. If you're in doubt, check whether there's any dirt build-up inside the air cleaner housing. If there is, it's a good idea to service the filter assembly; the procedure's given in the 12 000-mile Service Schedule.

3   Examine cooling system hoses

Although there may be no leakage of engine coolant, it's a good idea to check very carefully the condition of the hoses. Press and squeeze them, and check for signs of cracking or perishing. Renew any that even look as though they might give trouble in the future. More information is given in the 24 000 mile Service Schedule covering draining of the coolant and refilling the system.

4   Clean spark plugs

Pull off the spark plug leads; if you think you won't know where each one goes when you put them back, a little dab of paint on the cable or plug cap will identify each one – remember that No 1 cylinder's nearest the radiator.

Check that there's no dirt around the plugs which might fall into the engine, then remove each plug using the proper spark plug spanner. The plugs should be cleaned by a garage equipped with a sand-blasting machine which will remove the dirt far more effectively than you can with a wire brush (which may damage the surface of the insulator around the central electrode, and lead to misfiring). A spare set of plugs overcomes the inconvenience of having to walk to the garage; in this way you'll always have a spare set ready to be used.

Wipe the plug insulators with a petrol-moistened cloth, and check that the screw threads are clean. Check the electrode gaps using a feeler gauge of the specified thickness, and if necessary bend the outer electrode inwards to obtain it. Never try to bend the central electrode – all you'll achieve is a broken **59**

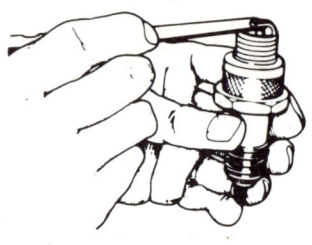

Checking plug gap with feeler
gauges

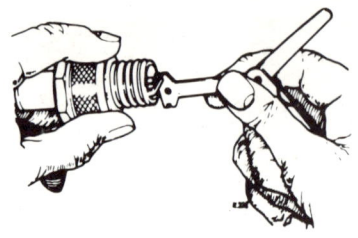

Altering the plug gap. Note
use of correct tool

Spark plug electrode conditions

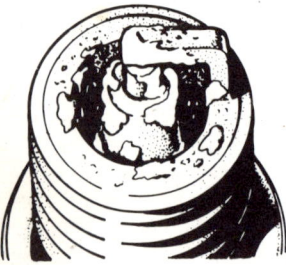

White deposits and damaged
porcelain insulation indicating
overheating

Broken porcelain insulation
due to bent central electrode

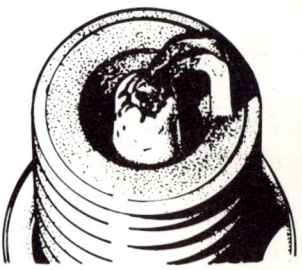

Electrodes burnt away due to
wrong heat value or chronic
pre-ignition (pinking)

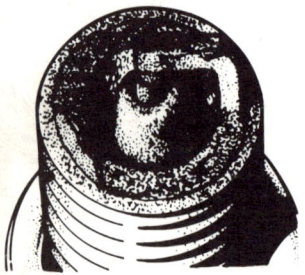

Excessive black deposits
caused by over-rich mixture or
wrong heat value

Mild white deposits and
electrode burnt indicating too
weak a fuel mixture

Plug in sound condition with
light greyish brown deposits

Spark plug maintenance

insulator. When the plugs are clean and reset, check that the seating on the block is clean and that the washer's on the plug. Apply a drop or two of oil on the plug threads then tighten them down firmly — don't overtighten them or you'll have difficulty in removing them next time.

Don't bother to fit the plug leads yet, because you'll need them off for the next check...

5   Clean contact breaker points and lubricate distributor

After a period of time, due to the sparking which occurs at them, the contact breaker points will need cleaning. A build-up occurs on one contact and a small crater appears on the other one; also the electrical resistance of the contacts increases. These things lead to starting problems and a general fall-off in the efficiency of the ignition system.

To clean the contacts, remove the spring clips and take off the distributor cap; next pull the rotor arm up and off.

Regal models will be found to be fitted with one of two types of contact breaker set, of either single or two-part construction.

Two-part contact set (Regal models): Unscrew the terminal nut, taking care that it doesn't drop inside the distributor, and remove the steel washer under it (if there is one). Remove the top flanged bush, and the condenser and low tension (LT) lead; you can now lift off the moving contact. Remove the fibre washer or lower flanged bush, then remove the screw and washer (don't drop them) and lift out the other contact.

Single part set (Regal models): On this type of contact set the moving and fixed contacts are joined together so you won't have any spacing or insulating washers to worry about. Removal is straightforward and is simply a case of removing the terminal nut, lifting away the low tension (LT) and condenser leads, and unscrewing the contact adjuster/retainer screw. The contact set can now be lifted away for cleaning or renewal.

Robin and Kitten models are fitted with a single part contact set but this is somewhat different from the type fitted to Regal models.

Single part set (Robin and Kitten models): Press the terminal end of the moving contact spring inwards to disengage the spring from the insulating piece attached to the terminal post. The condenser and low tension fly-lead can then be disconnected from the folded end of the spring. Remove the single screw securing the contact set to the distributor baseplate and then lift the contact set away.

Refacing contacts: To reface the contacts, rub them on a fine carborundum stone or fine emery cloth. Take care that metal isn't removed from one

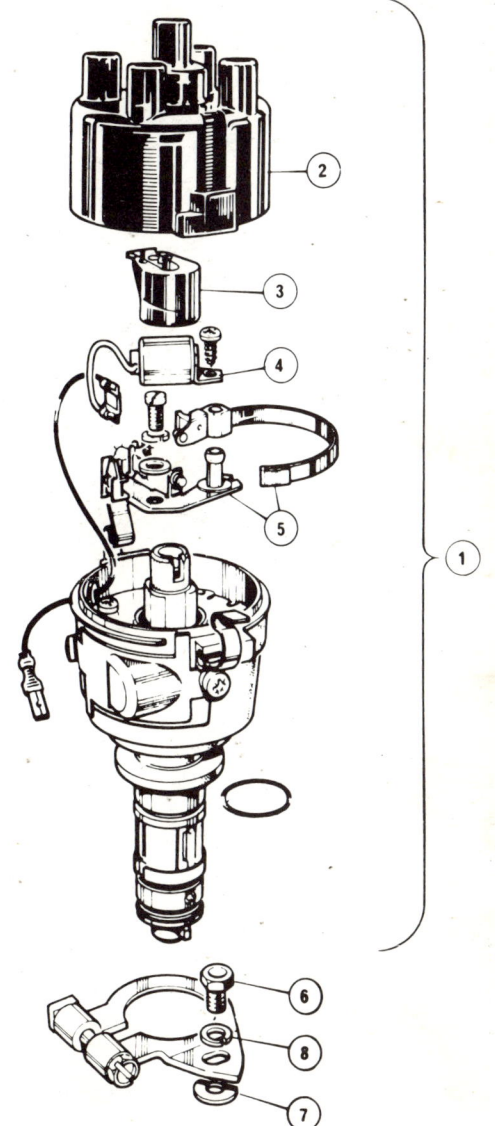

Typical exploded view of the distributor as fitted to Robin and Kitten models

1 *Distributor* 2 *Cap* 3 *Rotor* 4 *Condenser*
5 *Contact set (shown dismantled for clarity)*
6 *Clamp plate to cylinder block securing bolt*
7 *Spacer washer* 8 *Spring washer*

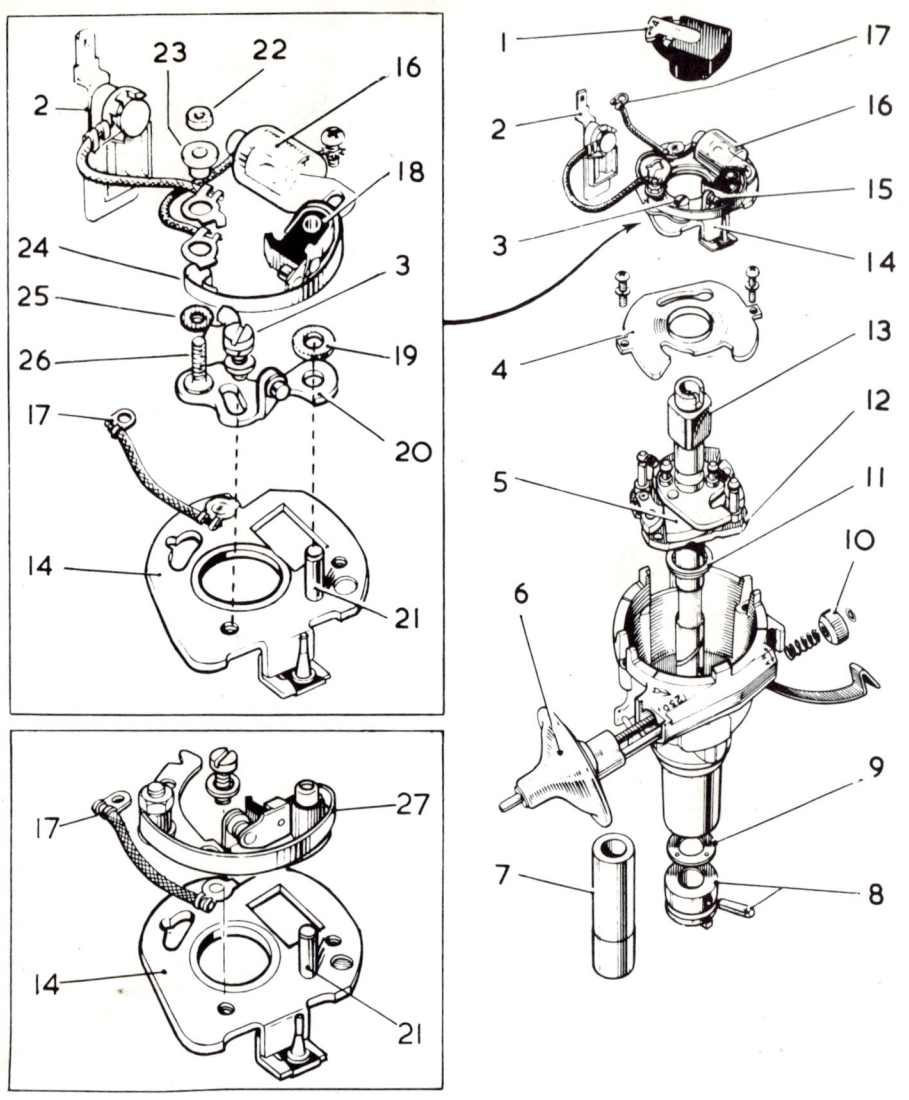

Exploded view of the distributor as fitted to Regal models
(Shown on lower left is the Quikafit single part contact set)

1	Rotor arm	*control unit*	15 Contacts	22 Nut
2	LT terminal	7 Bearing bush	16 Condenser	23 Shouldered
3	Fixed contact	8 Driving dog and	17 CB earth conn-	insulator
	plate securing	pin	ector	24 Movable contact
	screw	9 Thrust washer	18 Contact breaker	point spring
4	Contact breaker	10 Vernier adjust-	lever	25 Insulating
	baseplate	ment nut	19 Insulating	washer
5	Centrifugal	11 Distance collar	washer	26 Terminal pillar
	advance control	12 Baseplate	20 Fixed contact	27 Quikafit contact
	weights and	13 Cam	plate	breaker point
	mechanism	14 Contact breaker	21 Contact breaker	assembly
6	Vacuum advance	moving plate	pivot post	

edge of the contacts, because when they're fitted they need to be flat and parallel, or very slightly domed so that they touch at their midpoints. Make sure that the contact faces are very smooth when they've been rubbed down or they'll rapidly burn and wear.

Refitting is now the reverse of the removal procedure. Lightly tighten the securing screw, then select a gear and push the car a little so that the heel of the moving contact is on one of the peaks of the cam. Now, out with the feeler gauges again and select the size given in *Vital Statistics* for the points gap. Place the feeler between the contact faces and use a screwdriver in the notch to set the gap, rotating the screwdriver a little one way or the other as necessary. The feeler should be a firm sliding fit when the points are set; now tighten the screw and recheck the gap.

Apply a trace of Vaseline to the cam profile, one drop of oil to the moving contact pivot, two drops of oil to the felt lubrication pad in the top of the spindle, and three or four drops through the hole in the contact breaker plate to lubricate the advance weights.

Using a knife or a fine file, clean off any deposits from the rotor and metal electrodes in the distributor cap. Wipe the cap clean, and check that the spring behind the central carbon electrode is still effective. Wipe the plug leads and caps clean, and check that they're all in good condition; if there's any doubt, renew them without a second thought before they give you trouble. Now fit the rotor and cap to the distributor, and reconnect the plug leads in the correct order. Then start the engine (just to make sure that it does!)

Should it ever be necessary to renew the condenser (that's the silvery cylindrical object inside the distributor) this is a comparatively simple job. It's secured to the distributor baseplate by a single screw

Checking the contact breaker points gap using the correct size feeler gauge

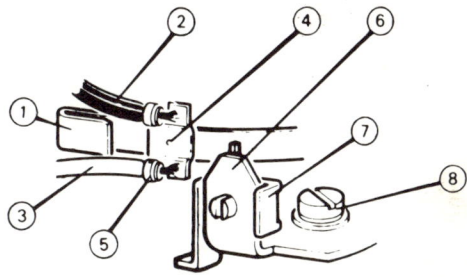

Detail of the LT connections of the distributor (as fitted to Robin and Kitten models)

1 Folded end of moving contact spring 2 LT fly lead (Black) 3 Condenser lead (Orange) 4 LT terminal 5 Cable clips 6 Terminal post 7 Nylon insulating piece 8 Fixed contact securing screw

Using a screwdriver to move the fixed contact when adjusting the contact breaker points gap

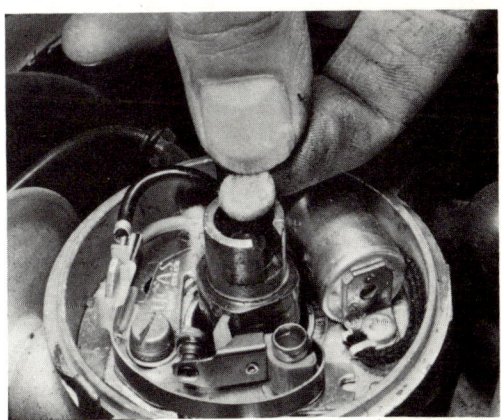

The felt lubrication pad (shown removed)

Internal view of the distributor cap showing the four metal electrodes and the central carbon electrode.

— the only point to watch is that the 'flying lead' is refitted correctly, so take a note of the set-up when you remove the old condenser.

6   Check ignition timing

As the contact breaker heel wears, or where a new contact set has been fitted, there may be a slight shift of ignition timing — that's the moment at which the spark occurs. Checking the timing statically (that's with the engine stopped) is easily done, and this method is described. If you want a more accurate setting, you must use a stroboscopic light (this is dynamic timing); a light will normally be supplied with operating instructions and you'll find it quite easy to use but, if you haven't got one, dynamic setting's a job for your Reliant dealer.

Ignition timing marks will be found at the front of the engine, where a datum mark is cast on to the face of the timing cover, while grooves cut into the edge of the crankshaft pulley represent TDC (top dead centre) and 10° BTDC (before top dead centre).

Remove the distributor cap and note in which position the rotor will be facing when the engine's firing on No 1 cylinder. This is easily done by finding out which segment in the distributor cap serves No 1 spark plug HT lead. Rotate the crankshaft in a clockwise direction until the datum mark on the timing cover aligns with the first cut-out (10° BTDC) on the crankshaft pulley. The second cut-out is the TDC mark.

Check now that the rotor points to the No 1 spark plug lead segment in the distributor cap. If it doesn't, you'll have to turn the engine crankshaft through 360 degrees and realign the timing marks. Now, with the timing marks correctly aligned, take a look at the

Correct alignment of the timing marks (10° BTDC). The other notch represents TDC

contact breaker points and observe whether they're closed, about to open or already open.

If the timing's correct the points will just (and only just) be opening. If the points have already separated an appreciable amount, the timing's said to be advanced or early. On the other hand if the points aren't ready to open the timing's said to be retarded or late.

Regal models are fitted with a distributor which has two methods by which the ignition timing can be altered. Minor adjustments can be made by turning the knurled vernier adjustment screw, but this has its limits. Major adjustments can be made by slackening the distributor clamp bolt and moving the distributor body in either direction. Note that turning the distributor body in the opposite direction to the rotation of the cam will advance the timing, and vice-versa.

Robin and Kitten models aren't fitted with a vernier adjustment screw and any alteration in the ignition timing must be achieved by slackening the distributor clamping bolt and moving the distributor bodily.

You may find it difficult to judge exactly when the points are opening, but there's an easy way round this if you've got a 12 volt inspection lamp with crocodile clips attached to the cable ends. If you haven't got an inspection lamp you can easily make something up.

Connect one crocodile clip to the distributor body or a good earth point, and the other to the moving contact spring, then turn on the ignition. At the instant of the points opening, the bulb will light up and remain alight until the points close again. You can now adjust the timing as described above until the bulb just lights up. When you're happy with the timing, tighten the clamp plate bolt, refit the distributor cap and that's another job done.

7 Check valve clearances

Valve clearances must be correct for the engine to breathe properly – that is, to take in the correct amount of fuel/air mixture at precisely the right moment, and then get rid of the exhaust gases. The procedure for checking on all models is similar, although there might be a slight difference due to breather pipe routing.

Undo the rocker cover securing nuts and lift the cover away; if it's sticking, a blow with the ball of your hand will shift it but don't be too brutal. Now briefly take hold of each rocker in turn – you'll notice that when rocked from side to side some of them will have some free play.

Rotate the crankshaft in the normal direction of rotation (remember how we did it for checking the contact breaker points?) until No 1 rocker has free movement and No 8 has no free movement at all.

Using the correct size feeler gauge (see *Vital Statistics*) slide it between the end of the valve stem and the rocker. If the clearance is correct, the feeler will be a firm sliding fit; if it's too tight or too loose, adjustment is needed. To adjust, slacken the hexagon locknut while holding the ball pin with a screwdriver to stop it turning. Now turn the ball pin with the screwdriver to obtain the correct gap, tighten the locknut and check again. Repeat this if necessary.

Having done No 1 valve the remainder can be done, preferably in the order given below, as it saves time and effort in rotating the crankshaft.

Valve fully open	Check and adjust
No 8	No 1
6	3
4	5
7	2
1	8
3	6
5	4
2	7

With the valve clearances all correct, it's a good idea to renew the gasket beneath the rocker cover. Take off the old one and make sure that the seating surface on the cylinder head and rocker cover are clean, then put the new one in place. Don't use gasket sealant – if necessary a little grease can be used to hold it in place. Refit the cover and pick up the nuts; don't overtighten them because the cover will distort and the cork gasket will be squashed out. Now run the engine, checking for oil leaks around the gasket.

8 Clean oil filler cap and connecting hose

The oil filler cap contains a wire gauze element and acts as a breather vent for the engine. On Robin and Kitten models the cap is vented to the carburettor via a rubber hose. The condition of this hose is important and if loose, split or perished, it can cause

Checking the valve clearances
1 Feeler gauge 2 Ball pin adjuster 3 Locknut

air leaks which will result in misfiring and erratic running.

The filler cap should be washed in clean paraffin and dried thoroughly. Before refitting the cap dip it in clean oil and wipe it thoroughly.

9 Check oil level in steering box (Regal and Robin models)

Remove the steering box level plug, and if oil just trickles from the hole everything's OK. Top up only if necessary with the correct grade of oil (refer to lubrication charts) and then refit the plug.

10 Check steering and front suspension for wear, and lubricate

The first part of this check needs a second person for assistance, so grab yourself a passer-by or borrow your mother-in-law for a few minutes. The weight needs to be on the front wheel(s), and if you haven't got an inspection pit, you'd better lift the car and lower the front wheels on to concrete blocks or ramps. Don't forget the handbrake and rear wheel chocks, or the car may move.

Now, with the able bodied assistant in the driver's seat, get underneath and take a good look at the entire steering system. Ask the assistant to move the steering wheel backwards and forwards until resistance is felt each way, then check for slackness in any of the steering ball joints. This will be seen mostly as up-and-down movement if it's there and, if it is, you'll need new balljoints, which is a job for your local Reliant man. You can let your assistant go now, and proceed with checking the suspension system.

Raise the front of the car so that the front wheel(s) is/are hanging free on the suspension. Grasp the wheel top and bottom, and try to rock it. If there's any movement, check where it's coming from. On Regal and Robin models this could either be wear in

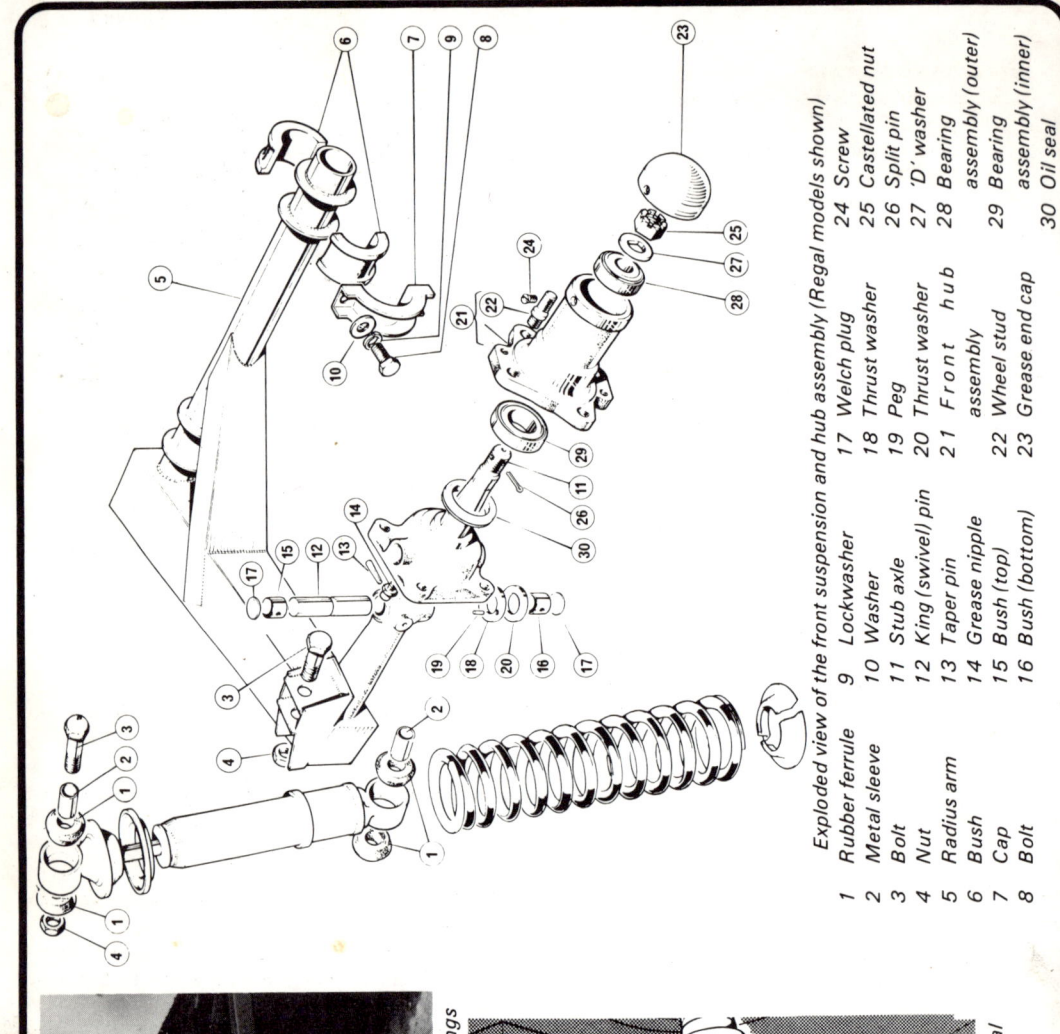

Exploded view of the front suspension and hub assembly (Regal models shown)

1	Rubber ferrule	9	Lockwasher	17	Welch plug
2	Metal sleeve	10	Washer	18	Thrust washer
3	Bolt	11	Stub axle	19	Peg
4	Nut	12	King (swivel) pin	20	Thrust washer
5	Radius arm	13	Taper pin	21	Front hub assembly
6	Bush	14	Grease nipple	22	Wheel stud
7	Cap	15	Bush (top)	23	Grease end cap
8	Bolt	16	Bush (bottom)	24	Screw
				25	Castellated nut
				26	Split pin
				27	'D' washer
				28	Bearing assembly (outer)
				29	Bearing assembly (inner)
				30	Oil seal

Rocking the roadwheel to check the wheel bearings

Steering box level/filler plug (Robin and Regal models)

1 Level/filler plug   2 Steering box adjuster

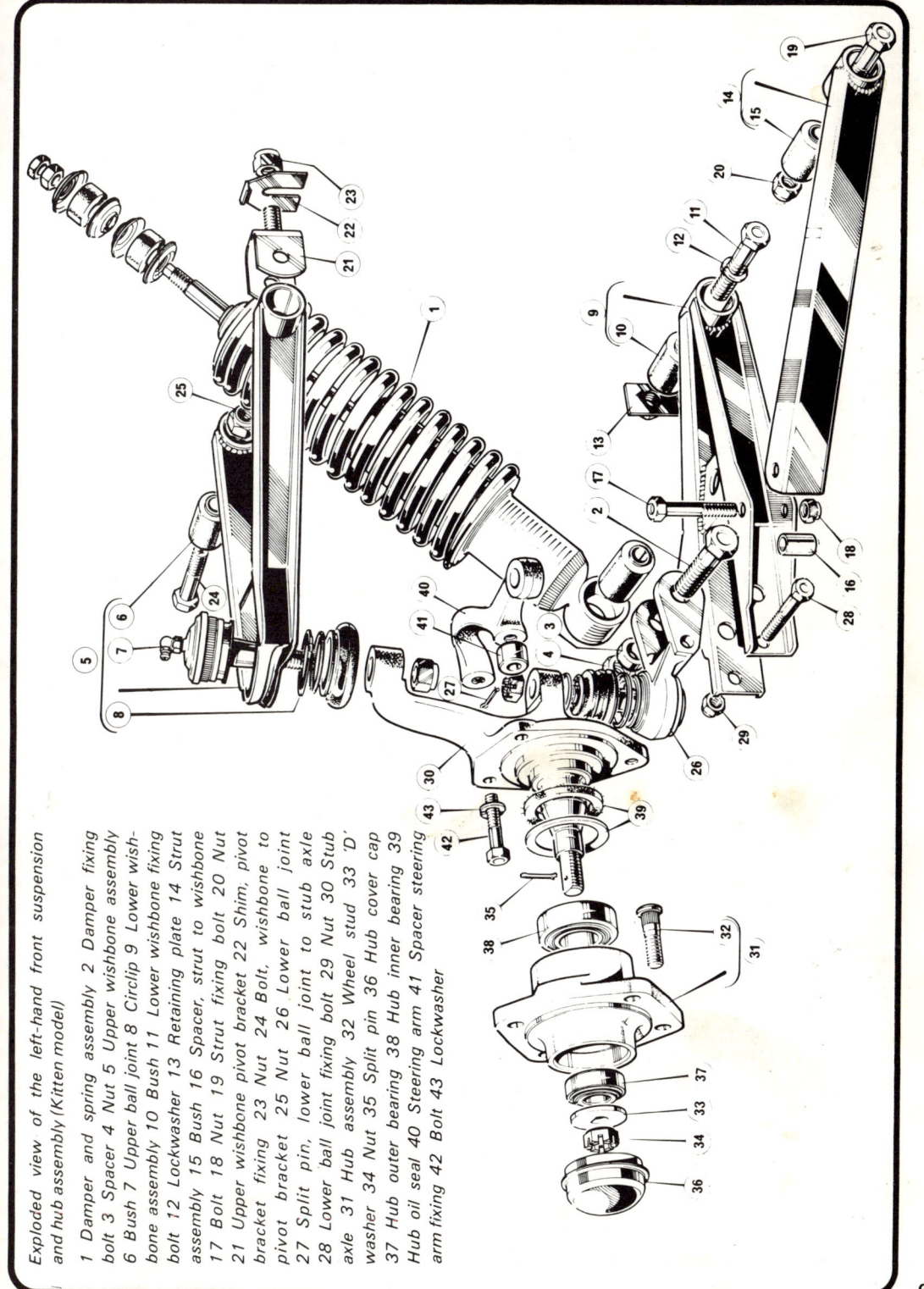

Exploded view of the left-hand front suspension and hub assembly (Kitten model)

1 Damper and spring assembly 2 Damper fixing bolt 3 Spacer 4 Nut 5 Upper wishbone assembly 6 Bush 7 Upper ball joint 8 Circlip 9 Lower wishbone assembly 10 Bush 11 Lower wishbone fixing bolt 12 Lockwasher 13 Retaining plate 14 Strut assembly 15 Bush 16 Spacer, strut to wishbone 17 Bolt 18 Nut 19 Strut fixing bolt 20 Nut 21 Upper wishbone pivot bracket 22 Shim, pivot bracket fixing 23 Nut 24 Bolt, wishbone to pivot bracket 25 Nut 26 Lower ball joint 27 Split pin, lower ball joint to stub axle 28 Lower ball joint fixing bolt 29 Nut 30 Stub axle 31 Hub assembly 32 Wheel stud 33 'D' washer 34 Nut 35 Split pin 36 Hub cover cap 37 Hub outer bearing 38 Hub inner bearing 39 Hub oil seal 40 Steering arm 41 Spacer steering arm fixing 42 Bolt 43 Lockwasher

the king pin and bushes or in the wheel bearings; on Kitten models the play will be either in the upper or lower balljoints or wheel bearings.

While checking the Kitten model cast your eyes over the rubber bellows at either end of the rack housing; if they're split or perished the oil in the rack assembly will escape and cause premature failure of the unit. If you have a leakage from these points it's generally because the fixing clips are slack.

Before lowering the car to the ground it's a good opportunity to lubricate the king pins/balljoints. Get out the grease gun and position yourself, one side or other, in front of the grease nipples. The exact positions of these are shown in the accompanying illustrations. Wipe the dirt from the nipples with a clean cloth, then give about four strokes of general purpose grease to each nipple.

Don't put too much in as it only seeps out; if you can't get any grease in, it means that the nipple's blocked or the component has sufficient grease in it already. If the nipple's blocked, it can be removed and soaked in petrol, or you can try holding it in a vice and forcing grease through it.

11 Check gearbox oil level

Robin, Kitten and later Regal models have a combined level/filler plug positioned approximately half-way up the left-hand side of the gearbox. Remove the plug, and if the oil level's correct it will just trickle over the lower edge of the plug hole.

On earlier Regal models a different checking procedure is required. Pull back the carpet from the region of the gear lever and slide the rubber grommet up the lever. Remove the two screws and lift away the metal plate. Pull out the gearbox dipstick and check the oil level as you would if you were checking the engine oil. Topping up is either through the dipstick hole or through a filler plug positioned next to the dipstick.

When topping up either type of gearbox use only the recommended grade of oil (refer to the lubrication charts) and avoid overfilling the gearbox.

12 Check clutch adjustment

While you're working in the region of the gearbox is the best time to check, and if necessary adjust, the clutch clearance. On Regal models pull the clutch pedal fully back and then, using a ruler, check the pedal free movement before any resistance is felt. The correct amount for Regal models is $\frac{1}{2}$ inch (13 mm). On Robin and Kitten models the cable's correctly adjusted when the clutch and brake pedals are level and there's approximately $\frac{1}{16}$ in (1.5 mm) free movement in the clutch operating arm at the trunnion.

If clutch adjustment's required this can be carried out as follows.

Regal (598 cc models): Undo the locknut and turn the barrel type adjuster to obtain the required amount of free play at the clutch pedal. When you're satisfied with the adjustment retighten the locknut, and adjust the self-locking nut on the threaded part of the operating arm so that the spring pressure is just sufficient to hold the adjuster nut firmly seated in the cupped end of the operating lever.

Regal (701 cc models): Undo the locknut and adjust the clutch clearance by turning the captive nut which is retained in the channel section. After making the necessary adjustment don't forget to tighten the locknut.

Kitten and Robin models: Pull back the inner clutch cable, releasing the adjuster nut from the trunnion block located in the clutch operating arm. Make the necessary adjustment by turning the adjuster nut until there's approximately $\frac{1}{16}$ inch (1.5 mm) free movement of the clutch operating arm at the trunnion.

13 Check propeller shaft condition and security, and lubricate

First of all check the security of the shaft flange bolts using a spanner. Now check the condition of the universal joints by grasping both parts of the joint and attempting to twist them in opposite directions. Any slackness between the two parts is an indication of wear in the joint. The sliding joint can be tested for wear using the same method. Finally apply the grease gun to the three nipples.

14 Grease handbrake system

All models have one or more grease nipple(s) on the handbrake system. Wipe the nipple with a clean cloth then apply a few strokes of the grease gun to each one. Wipe away any surplus grease afterwards. It's also essential to lubricate any moving parts of the handbrake system, especially where they're exposed to the elements.

15 Check rear axle oil level

The rear axle combined level/filler plug's located at the rear of the axle casing on Regal models, and on Robin and Kitten models it's on the left-hand side of the axle case.

Wipe any dirt away from the plug before removing it. If the oil level's correct the oil will just trickle over the edge of the hole. Top up if necessary with the correct grade of oil. Don't forget to refit the plug when you've finished and to wipe away any spilt oil.

16 Check all body, suspension and steering fixtures and connections

The easiest way around this task is to grab a

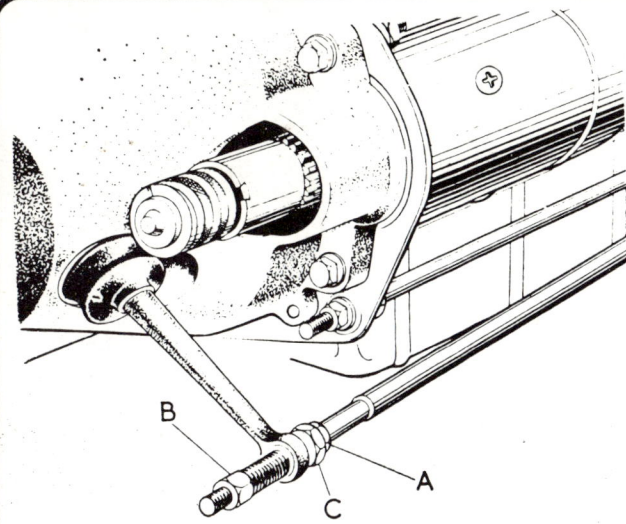

Clutch adjustment (Regal 600cc models)
A Locknut B Self-locking nut
C Adjuster nut

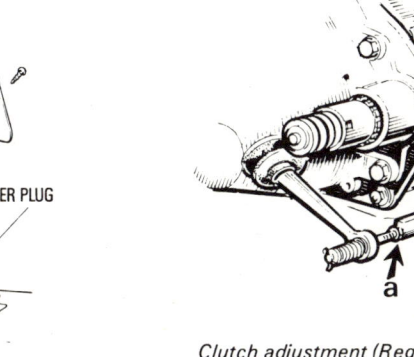

Clutch adjustment (Regal 700cc models)
A Locknut
B Captive adjuster nut

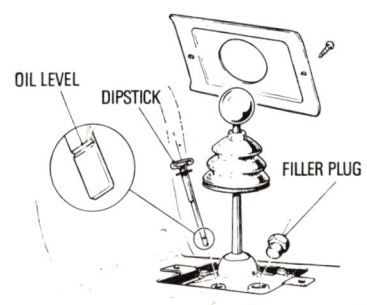

OIL LEVEL

DIPSTICK

FILLER PLUG

Checking the gearbox oil level (early Regal models)

Gearbox filler/level plug (arrowed) as fitted to Robin, Kitten and later Regal models

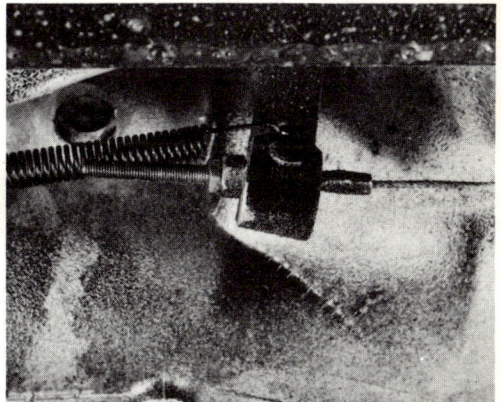

Clutch free-play adjustment point (Robin and Kitten models)

handful of assorted spanners and, starting from one end of the vehicle proceed to check the tightness of all the nuts and bolts which are anything to do with the systems listed in the heading. Don't exert too much force on the spanners or you could end up by shearing or damaging something.

17 Check condition of exhaust system

Visually examine the exhaust system and mountings. Remember that the exhaust system is now a part of the annual MOT test. Check the system for signs of corrosion and leaking joints. If you find any faulty mountings, replace them as soon as possible before they cause unnecessary strain and possible breakage of the system.

18 Examine all fuel and hydraulic lines for leakage, corrosion and damage

Examine the run of the petrol and hydraulic pipes, working from the back of the car forward. If you can't see everything at the back, do the job in two stages and raise each end of the car in turn for better access. The rigid pipes last a long time but can be damaged through accidents or stones being thrown up. The flexible pipes are the ones which deteriorate after a few years' service (as do all the rubber parts in the braking system, including the hydraulic cylinder seals).

Look for signs of dampness or bulging; they'll stand quite a lot of pulling about so don't think you'll cause any damage by checking - if you do, you've done yourself a favour because they were about to fail anyway. Don't forget any pipe runs in the engine compartment.

19 Check condition of brake shoes

Checking the brake shoes is simply a case of removing the road wheel, backing off the brake adjuster(s) and removing the brake drum. On Regal models the brake drum is retained by countersunk screws, but on Robin and Kitten models it's really the road wheel and nuts which keep it in position. If you experience difficulty in removing the drum, strike it evenly at several points around its rim with a soft mallet or block of wood.

When you've removed the drum examine the condition of the brake linings. If the linings are of the riveted type, they should be renewed where the lining material has worn down to within $\frac{1}{32}$ in (0.75 mm) of the rivet heads. Where the linings are of the bonded type the lining thickness must not have worn down to less than $\frac{1}{16}$ inch (1.5 mm).

Obviously, if your linings are almost worn down to these dimensions then it's only sensible to renew them now. **Note**: it's not advisable to attempt to reline your own brake shoes, and in fact service

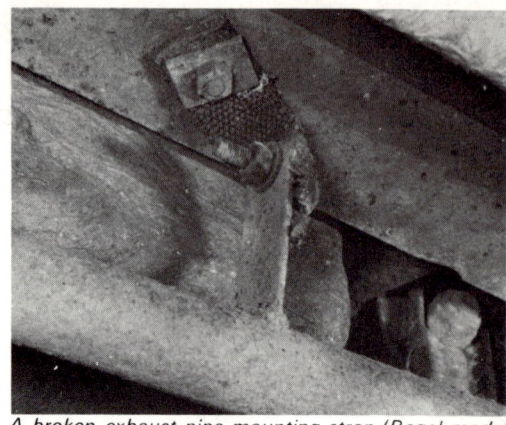

A broken exhaust pipe mounting strap (Regal model shown) will put undue strain on the entire exhaust system

exchange brake shoes are almost the same price as a set of linings so you won't save anything by doing the task yourself.

Examine also the hydraulic wheel cylinders; if they're weeping brake fluid then your best bet is to refit the brake drum and arrange for your Reliant dealer to rectify the fault as soon as possible. Description of this type of task is beyond the scope of this handbook, but it is covered in the Haynes Owner's Workshop Manual.

If your linings are OK, clean out the brake drum and dust off the linings with an old paintbrush. Don't blow the dust away by mouth or with a compressed air source, remember brake lining dust contains asbestos and is considered a health risk.

If your linings are worn down and need renewing then follow the procedures given below, which are applicable for all models. **Note:** Don't press the footbrake pedal when the brake shoes have been removed or the wheel cylinder pistons will be ejected.

Front brake shoes removal and fitting: First take note of the positions of the shoes and pull-off springs, a simple sketch is all that's required or alternatively you can scratch markings on the shoe webs. Now remove the shoe retainers. On Regal models these take the form of steady pins and spring clips and it's just a case of compressing the clip and then turning the steady pin through 90 degrees.

On Robin models the steady spring takes the form of a spring and a cupped washer which has a slot cut in it, but the same dismantling procedure applies. Kitten models, however, don't always have shoe retainers fitted, but where they are fitted they take the form of an inverted conical spring which is simply hooked into a hole in each of the wheel cylinder pistons and is easily prised out.

Now that you've (hopefully) released the shoe

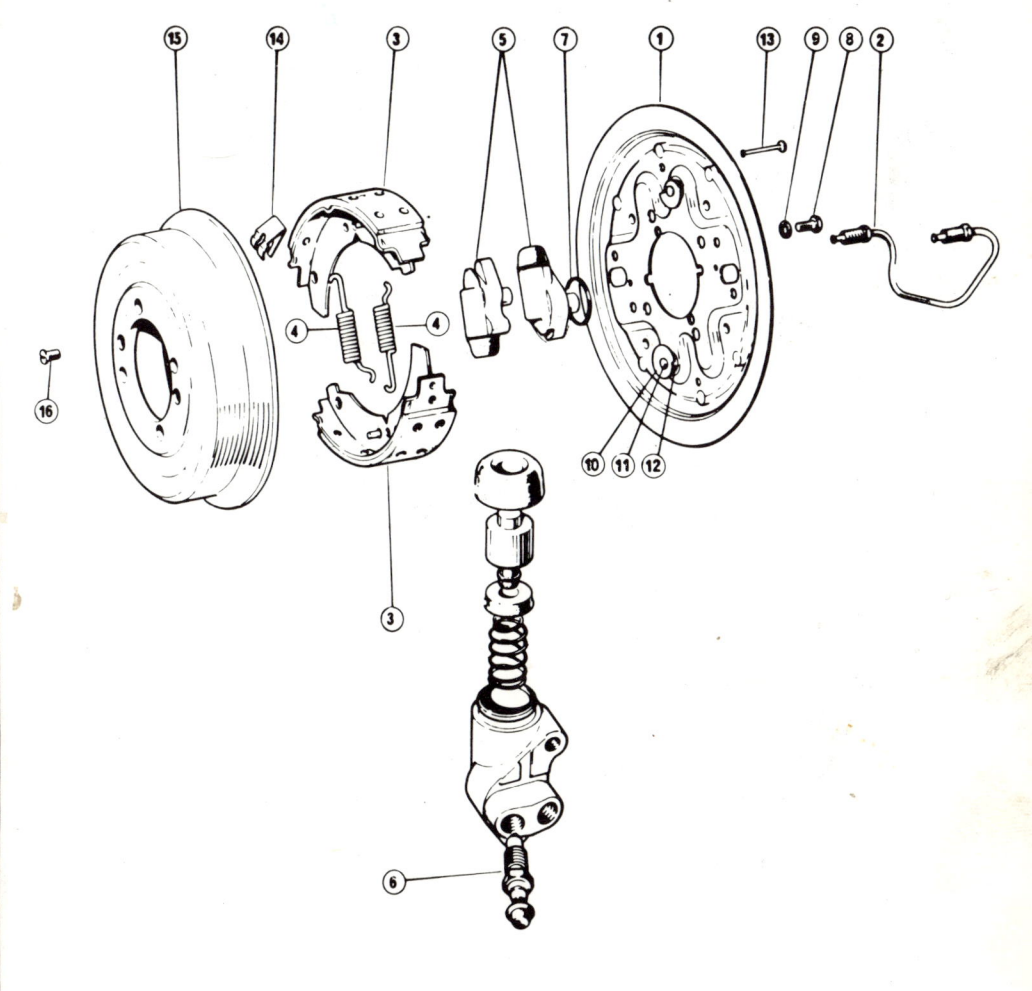

Exploded view of typical front brake assembly (Regal and Robin models)

1   Backplate
2   Bridge pipe
3   Lined brake shoe
4   B r a k e   s h o e
    spring
5   Wheel cylinder
    assembly
6   Bleed screw
7   Sealing ring
8   Bolt
9   Washer
10 Snail cam
11 S n a i l   c a m
    spindle
12 S n a i l   c a m
    spring
13 Peg
14 Clip
15 F r o n t   b r a k e
    drum
16 B r a k e   d r u m
    screw

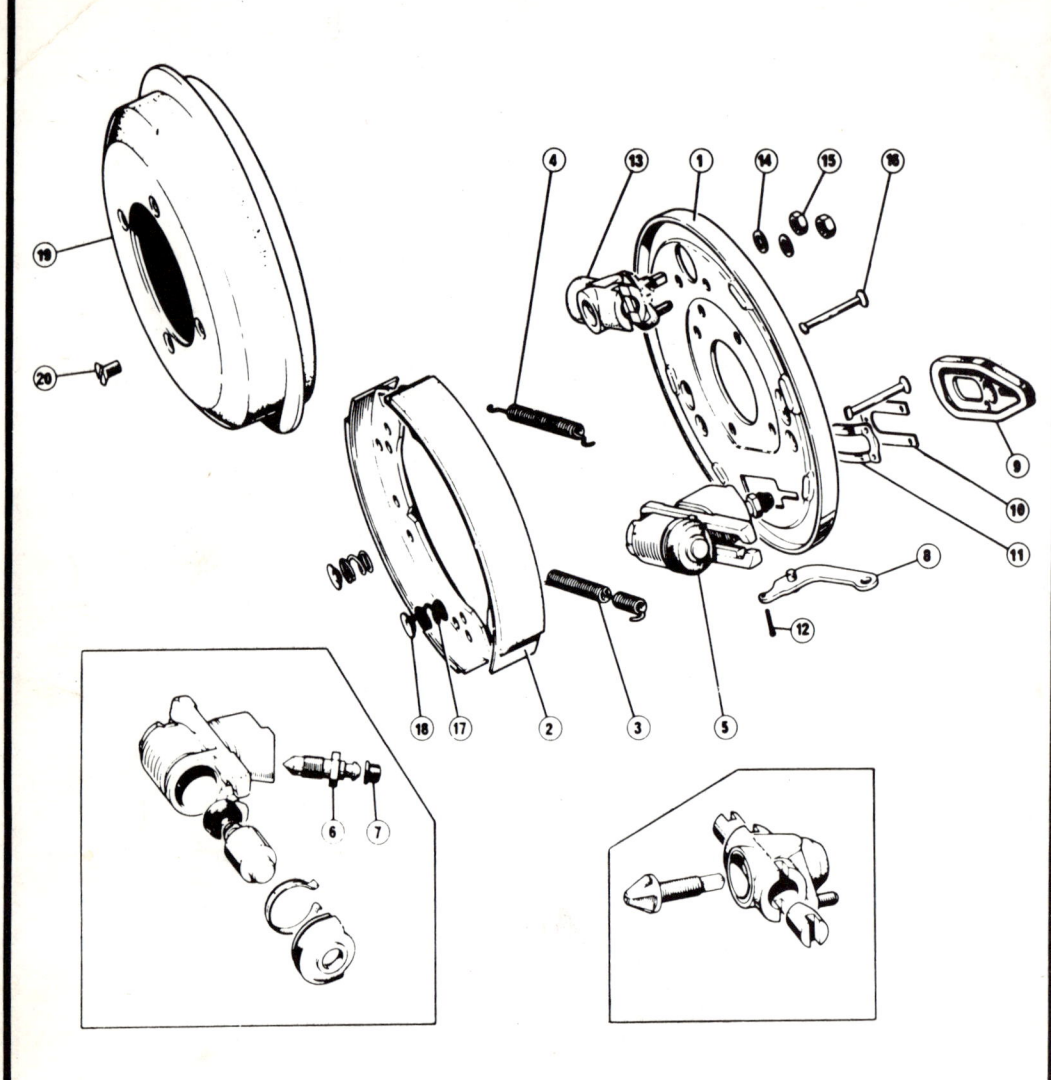

Exploded view of a typical rear brake assembly (Regal and Robin models)

1 Backplate assembly (left and right hand side)
2 Lined brake shoe
3 Shoe return spring, adjuster end
4 Shoe return spring, adjuster end
5 Cylinder assembly
6 Bleed screw
7 Dust cap
8 Lever assembly
9 Dust cover
10 Retaining plate
11 Spring plate
12 Split pin
13 Adjuster assembly
14 Washer
15 Nut
16 Peg
17 Spring
18 Cupped washer
19 Brake drum
20 Screw

The front brake assembly (Kitten model)

The rear brake assembly (Kitten model)

The rear brake assembly (Regal model)

retainers, carefully lever the end of the brake shoes from the grooves in the wheel cylinder bodies. Lift away both brake shoes from the backplate and lay them down on a clean surface. Before you do anything else, place a strong elastic band around each of the wheel cylinders to hold the pistons in place.

Clean down the backplate using a damp cloth, then lightly lubricate the brake adjusters with a proprietary brake grease. Lay the new brake shoes out in their correct positions and transfer the pull-off springs from the old shoes having cleaned and inspected them.

Remove the elastic bands from the wheel cylinders, place the new shoes (with springs attached) against the backplate, and locate the ends of the shoe webs in the grooves of the wheel cylinder bodies. Place a screwdriver under the web of each shoe, and carefully lever it out over the adjuster spindle and into the wheel cylinder piston groove.

Now refit the shoe retainers and then clean and refit the brake drum. The brake shoes can now be adjusted as described in the 3000 mile Service Schedule.

Rear brake shoes - removal and fitting: First take note of the positions of the brake shoes and pull-off springs, a simple sketch will do or alternatively you can scratch markings on the shoe webs.

Now release the shoe retainers, which are only to be found on Regal and Robin models. To do this depress the cupped washer to compress the spring beneath it, and then turn the steady posts through 90 degrees to release them. Pull out the split pin which secures the shoe to the handbrake lever (also only applicable to Regal and Robin models).

The brake shoes can be levered out from the slots in the wheel cylinder pistons and brake adjuster tappets using a screwdriver, but take care when disconnecting the brake shoe from the handbrake lever. Now place a strong rubber or elastic band around the wheel cylinder to retain the piston(s). Carefully clean the backplate with a damp cloth.

It's a good idea to dismantle the adjuster mechanism by removing the two tappets and the adjuster screw (removed from the front of the adjuster body). Clean these components, then reassemble them after applying a light coating of high-melting point grease. On Regal and Robin models the wheel cylinder's designed to slide a certain amount to operate the trailing brake shoe. If the wheel cylinder's seized, the leading shoe will do all the work and will wear out more quickly; use penetrating oil to free it.

Lay the new brake shoes out in their correct positions and transfer the pull off springs after having cleaned and inspected them. Remove the elastic band from the wheel cylinder, lift the assembled shoes up

73

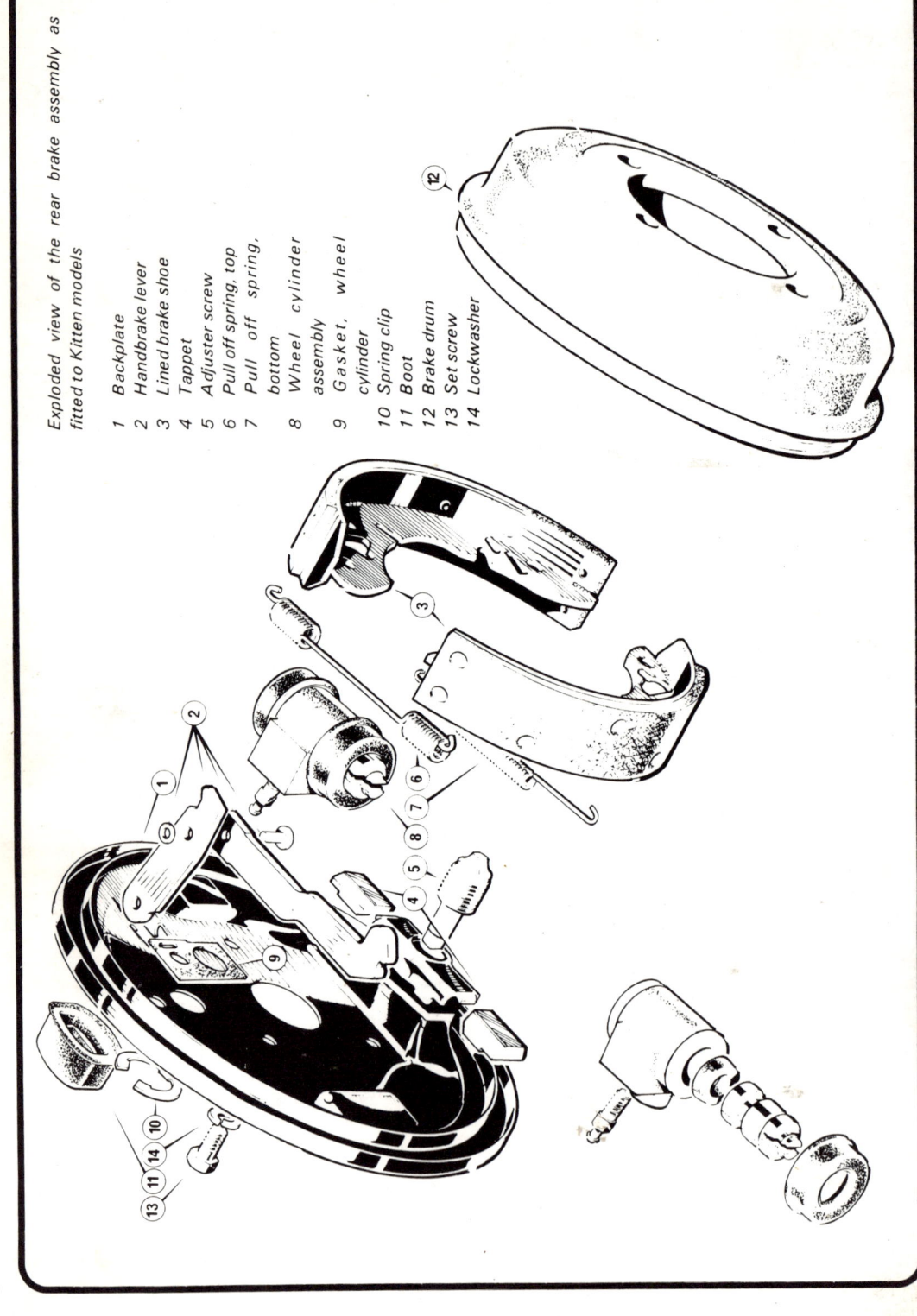

Exploded view of the rear brake assembly as fitted to Kitten models

1   Backplate
2   Handbrake lever
3   Lined brake shoe
4   Tappet
5   Adjuster screw
6   Pull off spring, top
7   Pull off spring, bottom
8   Wheel cylinder assembly
9   Gasket, wheel cylinder
10 Spring clip
11 Boot
12 Brake drum
13 Set screw
14 Lockwasher

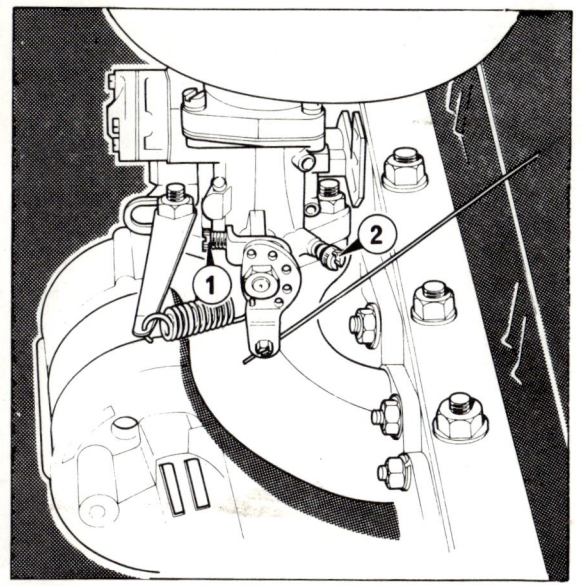

Zenith carburettor adjustment points (typical)
1   *Throttle adjustment screw*
2   *Volume control screw*

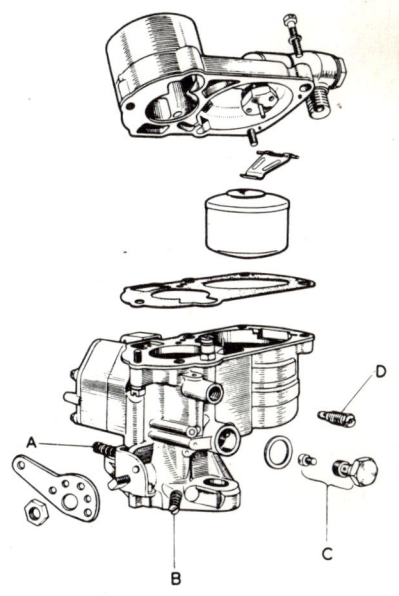

The main components of the Solex carburettor
A *Throttle adjustment screw*   C *Main jet*
B *Volume control screw*   D *Pilot jet*

into position on the backplate, and insert the end of the handbrake lever in the shoe web. Engage the tongues of brake shoes, one at a time, in the slots of both the adjuster and wheel cylinder piston. Check that the handbrake lever end is properly located in the shoe web cut out.

On Regal and Robin models the shoe retainers can now be refitted, along with a new split pin which is inserted through the hole in the end of the handbrake lever. The brake drums can now be cleaned and refitted. Finally adjust the brakes as described in the 3000 mile Service Schedule.

20   Road test the car

This you may think is the last task, but not quite - because the carburettor has yet to be adjusted, and this can only be done when the engine's at normal operating temperature. The road test therefore has two purposes: to warm the engine up and to test your previous handiwork.

Don't expect the brakes to be super-efficient if you've only just relined them, they won't reach peak efficiency until they've bedded in and been readjusted. Test the efficiency of the handbrake on a steep slope by applying it one notch at a time.

As the owner of the car you may feel a slight increase in engine performance, especially if your car was badly in need of a service, but don't expect miracles.

21   Check and adjust carburettor

Various types of carburettor have been fitted by Reliant to these models. If your carburettor is of the type designed to meet the DOE emission regulations, then Reliant recommend that all adjustments apart from idling speed are entrusted to a Reliant dealer. For the owner who wants to have a go, we've included instructions.

Note: Carburettor adjustments should only be made with the engine at normal operating temperature and after such items as air cleaner, spark plugs, contact breaker points, ignition timing and valve clearance have all been attended to.

Solex or Zenith carburettor

Slow running: This is set by adjusting the volume control screw. First of all start the engine and turn the throttle stop screw to obtain a fast tickover speed. Now screw in or out the volume control screw until all trace of 'hunting' or lumpiness disappears. Reduce the engine speed, if excessive, by turning the throttle stop screw. Readjust the volume control screw. Repeat the procedure until the desired tickover is obtained, but don't try to get too low a slow running speed. A fair indication of a suitable slow running speed is to watch the ignition warning light, which should just be glowing.

SU Carburettor

Slow running: Turn the throttle stop screw until the desired idling speed (900 rpm) is obtained. At this speed the exhaust note should be regular and even. If restoring the idling speed results in erratic running then the mixture requires adjustment. Reliant recommend that this adjustment is left to your Reliant dealer.

Fast idle (choke) adjustment: Pull out the choke control until the linkage is just about to move the jet. Start the engine and adjust the fast idle adjustment screw until the engine's idling at 2250 rpm (you'll need a tachometer to check this). Push the choke control fully in and then check with feeler gauges that there's a clearance of 0.040 in (1.016mm) between the end of the fast idle adjustment screw and the cam. When everything's set properly the choke control cable should be approximately $\frac{1}{16}$ in (1.6 mm) of free movement before it begins to operate the cam.

EVERY 12 000 MILES OR 12 MONTHS, WHICHEVER COMES FIRST

(In addition to the items listed in all the earlier Schedules).

The following tools, lubricants etc, are likely to be needed:

Torque wrench, feeler gauges.

Multi-purpose grease, air cleaner element (where applicable) set of spark plugs, front wheel bearing set and hub oil seal felts, pair of windscreen wiper blades, fuel filter (where applicable), split pins.

1   Renew spark plugs

The removal, gapping and refitting procedure is described in the 6000 mile Service Schedule (Item 4).

2   Service air filter assembly

Regal models: Early Regal models were fitted with an air filter which had an oil wetted gauze element. To service this type, first clean the exterior of the filter before removing it from the engine. Unscrew the clamp holding the filter to the carburettor, then split the unit by undoing the top screw. Remove the gauze and wash it in petrol or paraffin. Shake off the surplus, allow to air dry, then dip in clean engine oil. Drain off the surplus oil, wipe the interior of the filter body clean, then reassemble and fit to the carburettor.

Later Regal models were fitted with a paper element which is renewable. Clean the exterior of the filter before removing it from the engine. Unscrew the clamp holding the filter to the carburettor, then split the unit by undoing the clamp around the body. Remove the element and dust out the interior of the filter body. When fitting the new element, lightly

Adjustment points of the SU carburettor
A *throttle stop screw*
B *fast idle (choke) adjustment screw*
C *clearance (0.040 in) between fast idle screw and cam*

Removing the air cleaner assembly (Regal model)

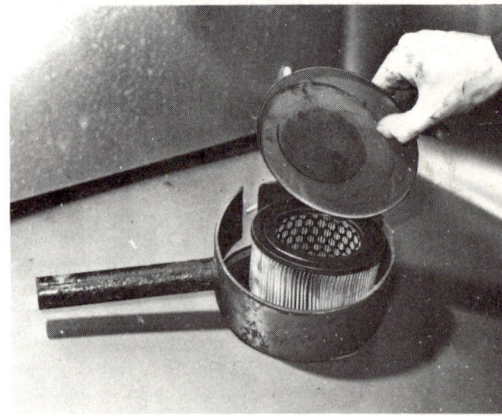

Dismantling the air cleaner assembly (Regal model with paper element)

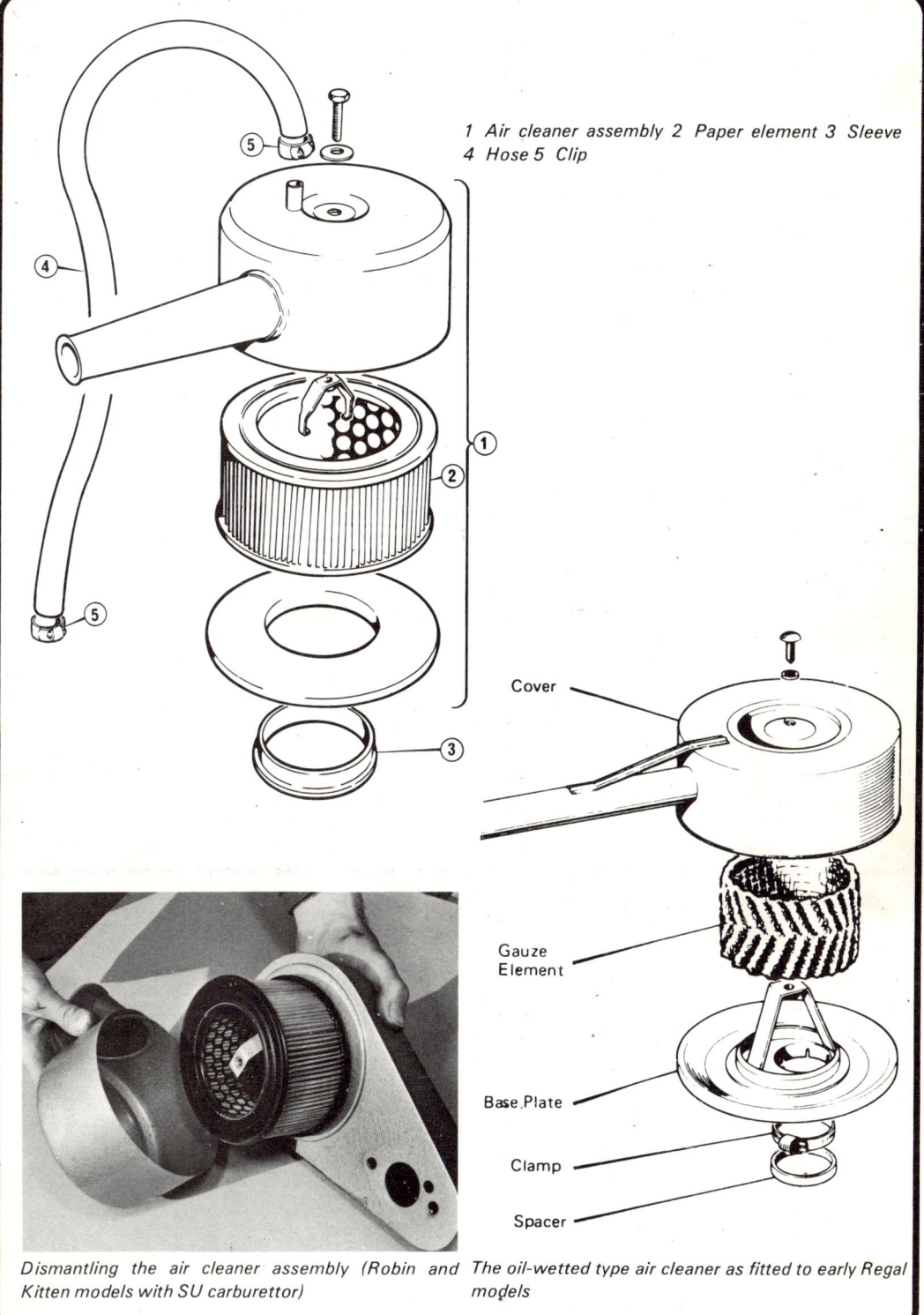

1 Air cleaner assembly 2 Paper element 3 Sleeve
4 Hose 5 Clip

Cover

Gauze
Element

Base Plate

Clamp

Spacer

Dismantling the air cleaner assembly (Robin and Kitten models with SU carburettor)

The oil-wetted type air cleaner as fitted to early Regal models

grease the plastic end faces before assembly. When refitting the filter to the carburettor, take care that the rubber sleeve is properly fitted with the filter right against the shoulder.

Robin and Kitten models: Robin and Kitten models are fitted with a renewable paper element. Clean the outside of the air filter body and then release the two spring clips or undo the central screw retaining the air cleaner body to the base plate. Lift away the air filter body followed by the old element. Clean the baseplate and the interior of the air filter body. Lightly grease the plastic ends of the new element and place it in position on the baseplate. Refit the air cleaner body and secure it in position with the two spring clips or central screw.

3   Check tightness of cylinder head, sump and manifold fixings

If you haven't got a torque wrench then this task must be entrusted to your local Reliant dealer. Don't be tempted to think that you can do it by guesswork — you could do more harm than good.

The points listed above should only be checked when the engine's **cold** and, in the case of the cylinder head, the nuts must be checked in the correct order (refer to the illustration).

Cylinder head nuts torque settings

Regal 598 cc	25 lbf ft (3.46 kgf m)
All other models	25 lbf ft (3.46 kgf m) except three nuts on spark plug side of head which must be tightened to 15 lbf ft (2.07 kgf m)

As for the sump and manifold fixings, you'll just have to check that they're tight, but don't use too much force on the spanner, socket etc or you may shear something off.

4   Renew windscreen wiper blades

With time, wiper blades deteriorate. They're affected by oil and fumes which collect on the windscreen, and the wiping motion wears them down. Annual renewal is the best method to ensure that they're always working satisfactorily and it's a straightforward operation.

Pull the wiper arm away from the windscreen and draw the blade out of the socket with a gentle outward pull. The end of the arm is inserted into the blade holder and the blade swivelled to lock the two together.

If the arm has worn at its pivot point then it should be renewed. To do this release the spring clip using a small screwdriver, then pull the end fitting from the splines. Refitting is straightforward but check the sweep action and reposition the arm on the splines if necessary.

5   Check headlamp alignment

This is not a D-I-Y job and should be left to your Reliant dealer or a garage which is equipped with the necessary apparatus.

6   Change fuel filter element

Some Reliant models are fitted with an in-line fuel filter which should be renewed at 12 000 mile intervals. The location of the fuel filter on Robin and Kitten models is on the frame side member just in front of the fuel tank. To remove the fuel filter, squeeze together the ends of the spring clips, pull the filter housing from the pipe line and extract the filter element. When installing the new element ensure

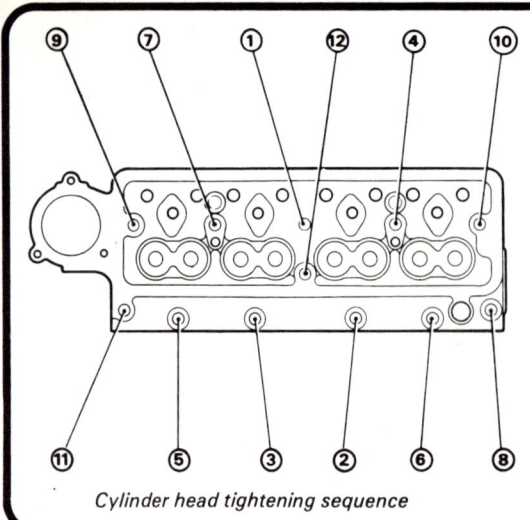

Cylinder head tightening sequence

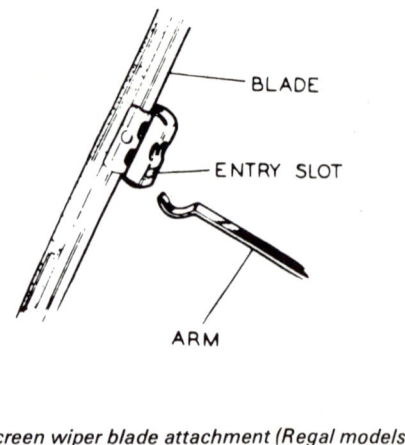

Windscreen wiper blade attachment (Regal models)

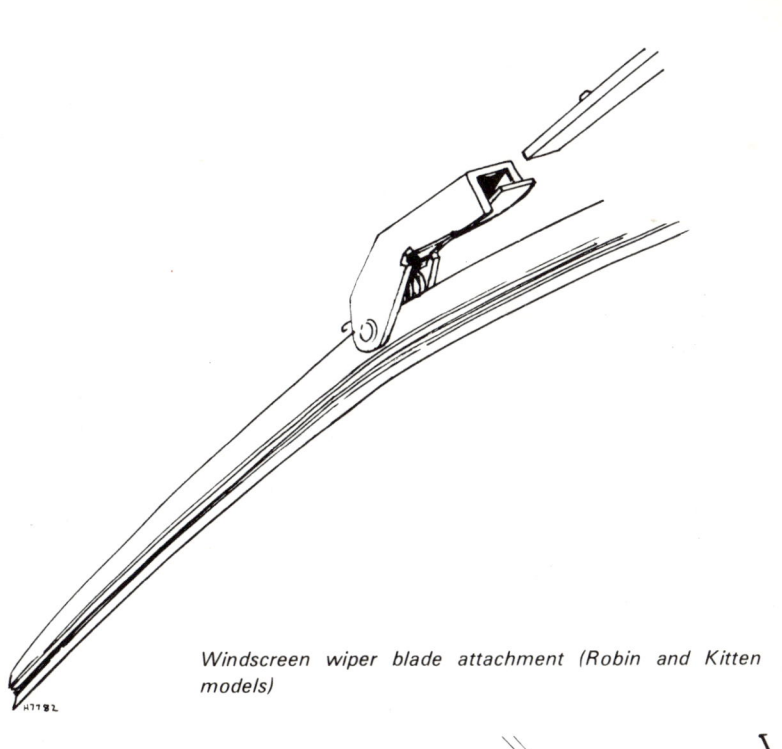

Windscreen wiper blade attachment (Robin and Kitten models)

RETAINING CLIP

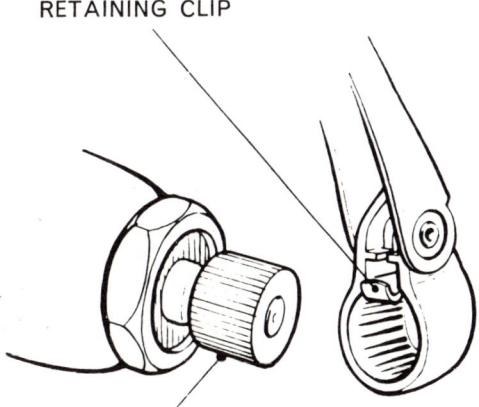

SPLINED DRIVING DRUM

Wiper arm attachment (all models)

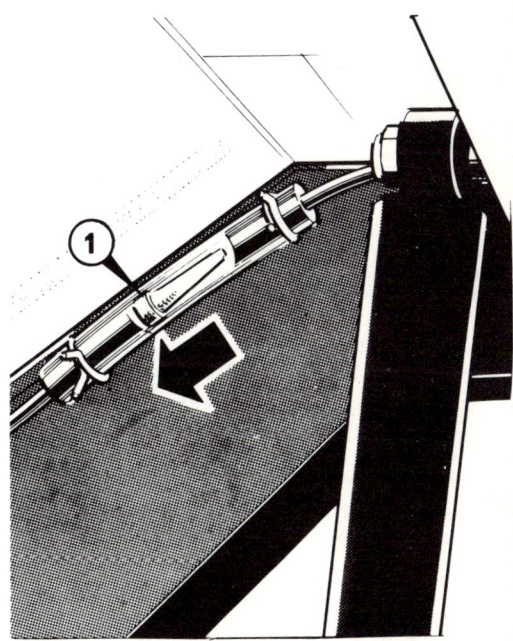

The in-line fuel filter as fitted to Robin and Kitten models
1   Filter element (Arrow shows direction of flow)

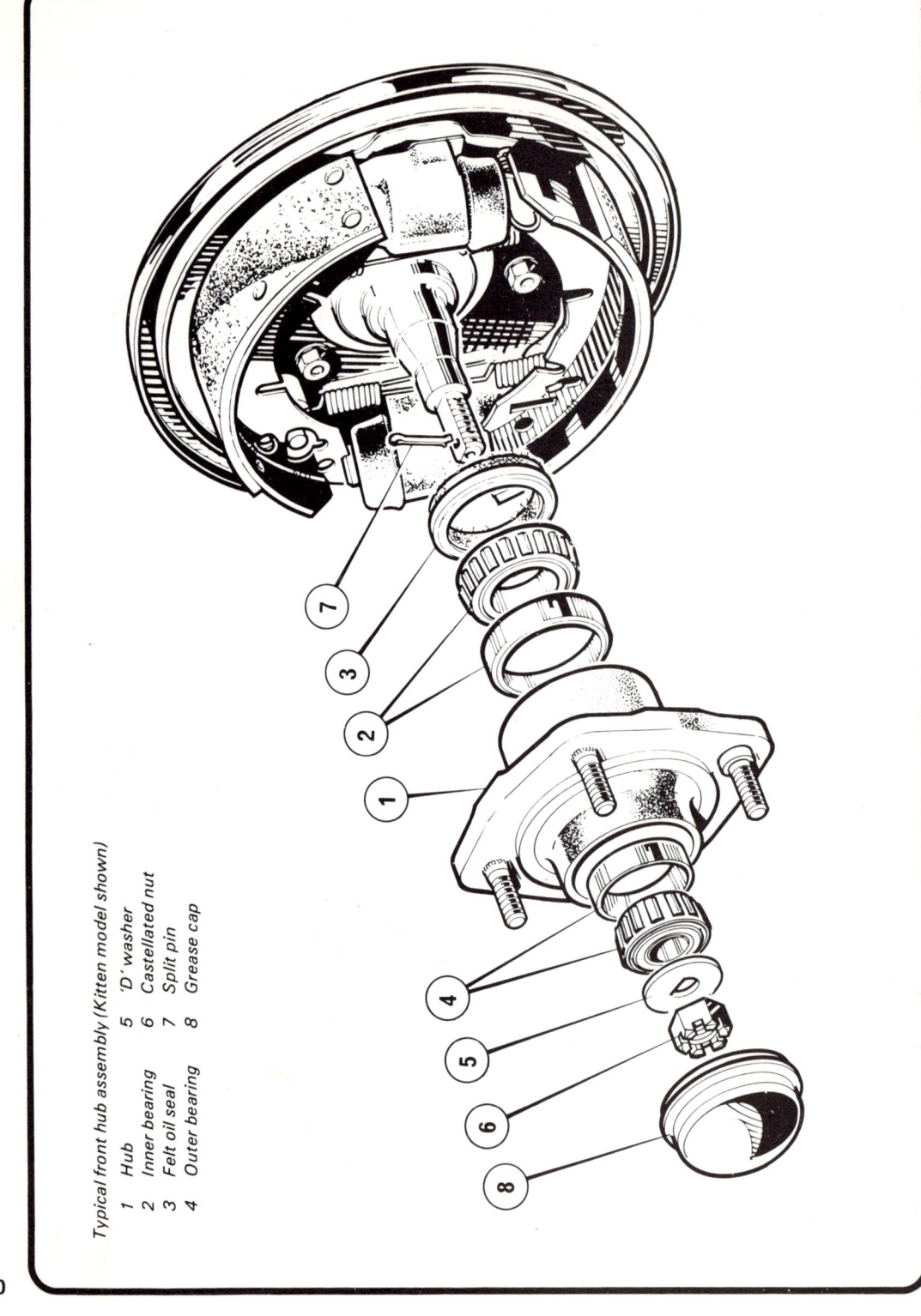

Typical front hub assembly (Kitten model shown)

1 Hub
2 Inner bearing
3 Felt oil seal
4 Outer bearing
5 'D' washer
6 Castellated nut
7 Split pin
8 Grease cap

that it's fitted as shown in the illustration.

Where there's an integral filter in the fuel pump, this should be removed for cleaning. (You can tell if your car has this type of pump fitted as the top cover is dome-shaped and secured by a single central screw).

Take out this screw (don't lose the washer) and carefully lift away the cover, sealing ring and gauze filter. Wash the filter in clean petrol and remove any sediment from inside the pump. When refitting, check that the sealing ring is sound. Don't overtighten the retaining screw or you'll distort the cover. Prime the pump by operating the side lever until no resistance is felt. Start the engine and check for leaks from the pump.

7 Change gearbox oil

The gearbox drain plug's located at the bottom of the casing. Before removing it, take out the filler/level plug at the side so you know you'll be able to refill the gearbox again! After draining the old oil, refit the drain plug and top up with fresh oil of the correct grade as described in the 6000 mile Service Schedule.

8 Clean rear axle breather

The rear axle of all models is provided with a breather which vents the axle and prevents any pressure building up within the casing, which could cause oil leakage from the pinion and half shaft seals. Use a piece of stiff wire to test the breather and to clear out any possible leakage.

9 Remove and check front wheel bearings

Raise the front of the car, support it on axle stands or packing blocks and remove the front road wheel(s). Now remove the front brake drum as described in the 6000 mile Service Schedule. The grease cap fitted to the end of the hub is retained by a screw on Regal models, but on Robin and Kitten models it's just a tight fit in the end of the hub and can be carefully levered out using a couple of screwdrivers.

The hub nut is prevented from unscrewing by a split pin, which can now be extracted using a pair of pliers. Robin models don't have a castellated type hub nut but use instead a castellated locking device placed over the top of a plain hub nut. Undo the hubnut, rock the hub from side to side, and extract the 'D' washer and outer bearing race.

The hub can now be slid off the stub axle and prepared for dismantling. Remove the felt oil seal and extract the inner bearing race. The hub can now be washed in clean paraffin or petrol, but don't wash the oil seal felt as you'll have to renew it anyway. After cleaning the parts, thoroughly dry them with a lint-free cloth and then inspect the bearing races and outer tracks.

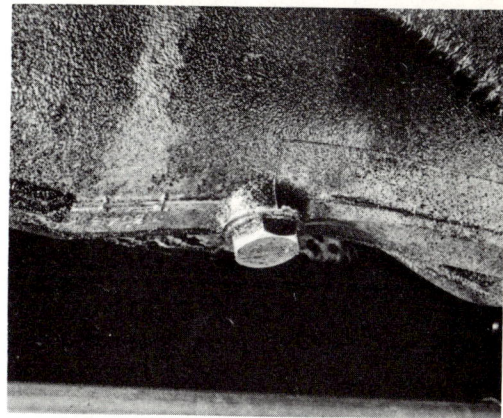

The gearbox drain plug

The hub grease cap removed (Regal model)

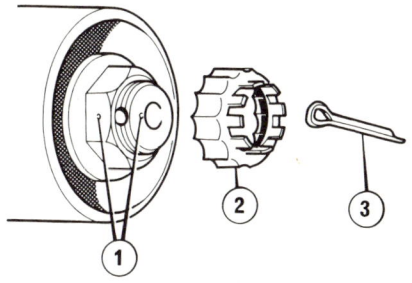

Front hub nut and fastener (Robin model)
1 Center punch marks 2 Castellated retainer 3 Split pin

Examine the bearings and outer tracks (these are still in the hub) for scoring, pitting, corrosion and overheating (a bluish colour). Brown staining can be ignored as this is a residue from the bearing grease. Ensure that the bearings run freely after cleaning. If both bearing sets are OK you can begin to repack the bearings and reassemble the hub as described in the next paragraph but ignoring the first part which deals with renewing the bearing assemblies.

If new wheel bearings are required it's important to make sure that both the inner and outer bearings are renewed as a complete assembly. This is because the inner bearing and outer track are mated together in manufacture, so it isn't possible to make up a good bearing assembly from salvaged parts or to swop parts around at will.

The bearing outer tracks can be drifted evenly outwards from the hub and the new ones installed. When installing the new outer tracks, ensure that they're fitted the correct way round (thin edges outwards). If you've fitted them wrongly you won't be able to install the bearing races.

To assemble the hub, first work general purpose grease into the bearing rollers, and smear it on the surface of the outer bearing tracks. Position the inner bearing race in the hub. remove the old felt from the oil seal. The new felt seal should be securely attached to the retainer using a suitable liquid jointing compound such as Hermetite. When the assembly has dried, the oil seal and retainer must be soaked in oil (squeeze out the surplus oil before pressing the oil seal into position on the hub).

Invert the hub and install the outer bearing race. Position the hub on the stub axle and refit the 'D' washer and hub nut assembly. Slowly tighten the hub nut by hand whilst rotating the hub. Continue tightening the nut until slight resistance is felt when turning the hub.

Now *slacken* the nut by 30 degrees ($\frac{1}{12}$ of a turn) or sufficiently to fit the new split pin. If you use this method of adjusting the hub nut you won't have any fear of overloading the bearings.

Before refitting the end grease cap, smear a little grease inside it, but don't overfill it as you'll have difficulty in refitting it. The remainder of the reassembly procedure is the reverse of the dismantling sequence.

EVERY 15 000 MILES OR 15 MONTHS, WHICHEVER COMES FIRST

(in addition to the items listed in the Weekly and 3000-mile Schedules)

The following tools, lubricants, etc likely to be needed:

Rear axle drain plug spanner (Regal models only), oil can.

2 pints of rear axle oil (Regal models only).

1 Lubricate dynamo rear bearing (Regal models only)

The dynamo rear bearing should be lubricated by injecting a few drops of oil through the hole in the centre of the rear end plate.

2 Drain rear axle (Regal models only)

Remove the rear axle drain and filler plugs and drain out the oil into a suitable receptacle. After the axle has drained, refit the plug and top up the axle through the filler plug hole, using the correct grade of gear oil, until it just begins to run out of the hole. Refit the filler plug and wipe up any spillage.

EVERY 24 000 MILES OR TWO YEARS, WHICHEVER COMES FIRST

(in addition to the items listed in the first four Schedules)

The following tools, lubricants, etc are likely to be needed:

Miscellaneous spanners and screwdrivers.
Antifreeze, distributor rotor, condenser and cap.

1 Renew distributor rotor, condenser and cap

We've attended to most of the things in the ignition system at regular intervals but the rotor, cap and condenser haven't really been included apart from keeping them clean. To keep the system in perfect tune, these items should now be renewed also. The plug leads we've been keeping an eye on, but if your car has the carbon fibre type leads (ie. they're not wire inside the insulation), these too should be renewed. Fitting all these items is straightforward - those little screws inside the distributor cap retain the HT leads, and the condenser has one securing screw.

2 Renew antifreeze in cooling system

The antifreeze should be renewed every two years and the system flushed through just to make sure that it will be able to do its job properly. To drain the system, place a suitable container handy at the base of the radiator (something like the plastic washing up bowl used for draining the engine oil will do), then remove the drain plug or open the drain tap (where there is one) or detach the radiator bottom hose. The coolant will start to flow out and now, if the radiator cap is removed and the heater control moved to the 'Hot' position, will flow out much faster.

When the initial flow has stopped, remove the cylinder block drain plug, to drain the block. When all the coolant has drained get a can of water or a hosepipe, and run water through the system to remove any sediment that may be present. A proprietary flushing compound can be used if you've

The rear axle drain plug (arrowed) (Regal model)

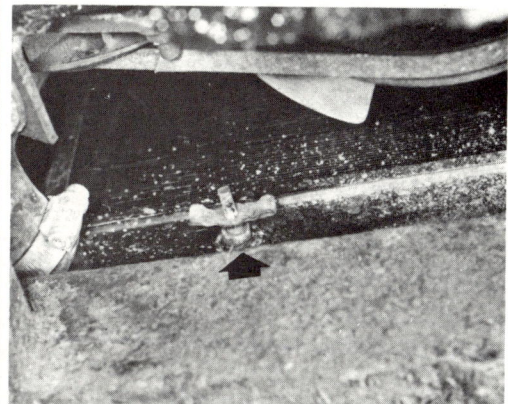

The radiator drain tap (Regal model)

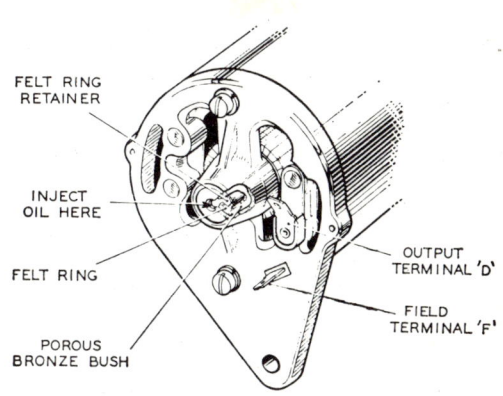

FELT RING RETAINER

INJECT OIL HERE

FELT RING

POROUS BRONZE BUSH

OUTPUT TERMINAL 'D'

FIELD TERMINAL 'F'

Dynamo rear bush lubrication point (Regal models only)

The cylinder block drain tap (Regal model)

The cylinder block drain plug (Kitten and Robin models)

any suspicions of the system being blocked, but follow the maker's instructions.

When you're satisfied that the system's clean, refit the drain plug(s) and turn off the drain tap (or refit the bottom hose), but leave the heater control at 'Hot'.

It's not absolutely essential to use antifreeze when refilling the system, but if you don't, Reliant recommend that you use a solution of Reliant Coolant Inhibitor 'R' (part No 10374) to maintain the system free from corrosion. If you use antifreeze, select a type which has corrosion inhibitors and is also suitable for aluminium engines. Antifreeze can stay in the system for two full years before it has to be drained out and you can even leave it in during the warmer weather.

The accompanying table can be used as a guide to calculate the quantity of antifreeze required for a given amount of protection.

Having decided how much you need, the antifreeze can be poured straight into the radiator followed by enough water to fill it. Run the engine at a fast idle to let the mixture circulate; as this happens the level may fall as airlocks are displaced. then will fall quite sharply when the thermostat opens. Finally top the radiator up and fit the cap.

Just to check that there are no air locks, use the car on the road for a short distance, then stop and allow the engine to cool, and recheck the coolant level.

EVERY 36 000 MILES OR 3 YEARS, WHICHEVER COMES FIRST

(in addition to the items listed in the first four Schedules)
1   Renew brake fluid and all rubber parts in the brake hydraulic system.

This is a job for your Reliant dealer and is beyond the scope of this Handbook. Research by the UK's largest manufacturer of brake fluid has shown that, because of its tendency to absorb moisture, this fluid can become dangerously unserviceable in a comparatively short time. Its capacity to resist vaporisation (caused by the heat generated during braking) is greatly reduced and the likelihood of 'vapour lock' occurring in the braking system is correspondingly increased.

This could lead to complete brake failure, as could the deterioration which gradually takes place in

the rubber hoses, seals etc. So don't neglect this task - it's for your safety as well as everyone else's.

OTHER REGULAR MAINTENANCE

If you've carried out the procedures we've described so far, at more or less the prescribed intervals of time or mileage, then you'll have gone a long way towards getting the best out of your Regal, Robin or Kitten in terms of both performance and long life. That's the good news. The other kind is that there are always other areas, not dealt with in the regular servicing schedules, where neglect can spell trouble.

We reckon a bit of extra time spent on your car at the beginning and end of the winter will be repaid in terms of peace of mind and prevention of trouble. The suggested attentions which follow have therefore been divided into Spring and Autumn sections - but there's nothing to prevent you doing them more frequently if you like!

SPRING

We've put this one first as it's less depressing than Autumn - though there's probably more work involved.

Underside of car

In Spring, we venture to suggest, the owner's fancy lightly turns to thoughts of cleaning off all the accumulated muck of the winter from underneath the car. Without a shadow of doubt, the best time to clean underneath is the worst from the discomfort point of view - that is, when the car has been driven in the wet and all the dirt's nicely softened up. So let's talk first about the easier way out — steam cleaning or pressure washing. These are not D-I-Y jobs, and can only be done at larger garages, usually those which undertake body repair jobs. You may feel this method is unnecessarily expensive, but it's generally preferable to grovelling about underneath and getting filthy and uncomfortable doing it yourself. However, for the owner who really wants to do it by hand, here goes…

You'll need paraffin or a water soluble solvent, water (and preferably a hose) a wire brush, a scraper and a stiff bristle brush.

To start with, jack the car up as high as possible, preferably at one side or one end. For your own safety, support it on ramps or concrete/ wooden

		Antifreeze requirements table			
Commences freezing at		Solution	Quantity of antifreeze to use (pints)		
°C	°F	%	Regal	Robin	Kitten
−9	16	20	1.40	1.00	1.30
−13	9	25	1.75	1.25	1.63
−16	3	30	2.10	1.50	1.95

Typical example of chassis rust

blocks, and chock the wheels which are on the ground. Unless both rear wheels are raised, also apply the handbrake.

Now get underneath (you've put if off as long as you can!) and cover the brake drums with polythene bags to prevent mud and water getting into them. Next loosen any encrusted dirt and, working from one end or one side, scrape or brush this away. The paraffin or solvent can be used where there's oil contamination. After all the brushing and scraping, a final wash with the hose will remove the last of the dirt and mud.

While you're underneath take a good look at the chassis frame for signs of rusting, and if you find any have a word with your local Reliant dealer or body repair shop before things get too bad.

Bodywork

This too will have suffered from all the muck and debris that's around during the winter, and there's no better time to wash it thoroughly and check for chips, scratches and rust blemishes. These repairs are covered in *Body Beautiful*.

After the touch-up paint has thoroughly hardened, it's worth giving the car a good polish to prepare it for the long hot summer ahead (well, there's no harm in hoping!) If you're really feeling energetic you could do the interior as well but the most important cleaning jobs are now done.

AUTUMN

With winter on the way, your car's electrical system is going to take much more of a beating than it has during the last few months. Now - and not one dark night miles from anywhere in a snowstorm - is the time to check the vital components. Where other Sections or Service Schedules are referred to in brackets, the detailed procedure is described there.

Battery

Ensure that this is topped up correctly *(Weekly Schedule)*.

Check and clean as necessary *(3000 miles)*.

Fan belt

Check and adjust tension or renew as necessary.

Lights

Check operation *(Weekly Schedule)*.

Renew any failed bulbs *(In an Emergency)* or check for faults as necessary *(Troubleshooter 6)*.

Wipers/Washers

These are going to get a lot of use so check the wiper arms and blades.

Top up washer reservoir *(Weekly Schedule)* and check operation.

Cooling system

Check all hoses *(6000 miles)*.

Drain, flush and refill system with new antifreeze mixture if necessary *(24 000 miles)*.

Tyres

Check tread and condition *(Weekly Schedule)*. Remember that you may well be driving in slippery conditions.

Bodywork

Finally, if you've got any energy left, wash the car and polish it thoroughly to help protect the finish against the winter elements.

Body Beautiful

A car always seems to go that much better when it's clean - whether or not this is purely psychological is open to argument. What can't be denied is that a car with clean bodywork and tidy interior generally gives the owner more satisfaction and pride of ownership than one that's allowed to deteriorate in both looks and value. If a car's in good all-round condition when you buy it, then there isn't too much effort involved in keeping it that way. But if your Reliant was obviously neglected by its previous owner(s) then a little extra effort is required to restore some of the former 'glory' provided it isn't too far gone when you start!

Some people regard car cleaning as one of the joyful aspects of ownership, while others look on it as a tedious task and a necessary evil. If you fall into the latter category, then the best plan of action is to do a little each week, dividing the job into sections. In this way you'll at least maintain a reasonable standard of appearance and break up the monotony of the job.

The really keen types won't only have the interior and bodywork dazzling, but will also keep the engine free of dirt and oil. Though you may be horrified at the idea, it's not a bad one when you think of it. For one thing, if you do carry out any repairs on the engine or surrounding components, the job will be made much easier and more pleasant just because you'll keep yourself cleaner and be able to see what you're doing. Another point is that any oil or water leaks can easily be traced at an early stage and rectified before they get really serious.

If you've only recently got your Reliant and the engine's barely visible through the coating of muck, the easiest way to clean it, as with the underside, is to take it along to a garage equipped with a steam cleaner. For a small cash outlay, this will save you a lot of time and effort, and thereafter the engine can be

wiped clean using a rag lightly dampened in paraffin.

If you decide to clean it by hand, scrape off the worst of the dirt, then brush on a solvent such as Gunk or Jizer and hose off the remainder but remember to cover the ignition leads, distributor, coil, generator and carburettor with polythene sheeting or bags or the engine will be difficult to start again and the charging system will go haywire.

If you've bought this Handbook intending to do all the routine servicing of your car yourself, then you'll surely want to keep the bodywork and inside of the car looking good too. And for anyone who doesn't here's how to do it anyway...

It's always a good idea to clean the interior first; this way you won't get the dust all over your nicely polished exterior - or the car's! Begin by removing all the contents, not forgetting the odds and ends in the pockets and glovebox. Then take out all the mats and carpets, which should be shaken and brushed, or better still vacuum cleaned. If they need further cleaning this can be done with a carpet shampoo, but let them dry thoroughly before you put them back. Any underfelt should be taken out and shaken too, but don't try washing this or it may end up in rather more pieces than you started with.

If the carpets should just happen to be in such a bad state of decay that they don't merit cleaning, why not get yourself a decent set of replacements? You can get kits tailored for your particular model from the specialist firms, and they're quite reasonably priced.

The inside of the car can now be cleaned with a brush and dustpan, or again preferably, a vacuum cleaner. If the flex on the Hoover won't stretch to the car (and the car won't squeeze through the front door!) it might be worth thinking about investing in one of the small 12-volt hand vacuums which can be attached to your car battery - your accessory shop can probably show you one.

Seat and trim materials can be wiped over with warm water containing a little washing-up liquid, but for best results (particularly if they're very dirty) use one of the proprietary upholstery cleaners such as Decosol, which are specially made for the job. An old nail brush will help to remove any ingrained marks, but don't splash too much water about and do wipe the surface dry afterwards with a clean cloth, leaving the windows open to speed up drying. The carpets can be put back when they're quite dry, making sure that they're properly fitted around the controls etc.

You have to be careful about cleaning car windows, especially the windscreen, with some household products as these can leave a smeary film. Water containing a few drops of ammonia is probably best, but any stubborn marks and smears can be removed with methylated spirit, finished off with a chamois leather squeezed as dry as possible.

Just in case you should think that's it, there's still the boot or load area to be considered. Take out all that collection of junk that seems to have grown every time you open the lid, and get busy with brush or vacuum cleaner again. While you're at it, if you must carry all that stuff around, now's the time to try and stow it so it doesn't rattle any more!

Now you can pause for a moment – make a well-earned cup of tea perhaps, and take a critical look at the interior. Are there any nicks or tears in the seats or other trim? Is the headlining drooping or peeling? Some excellent products can now be obtained for repairs such as these. One of the most useful is probably the vinyl repair kit, which comes in various colours and consists of a quantity of 'liquid vinyl' and some sheets of texturing material.

The liquid's applied to a split or hole in a plastic seat or piece of trim, smoothed like body filler, and allowed to set. It's then blended into the surrounding area by selecting the best matching pattern from the graining material supplied, placing this over the repair and rubbing with a hot iron; the pattern is then embossed into the repair area. This type of repair's equally successful, incidentally, on vinyl roofs if your car happens to have one.

For larger splits or tears it may be necessary to cut a piece of matching material from somewhere that doesn't show, apply some suitable adhesive to it and work it under the edges of the tear, pressing these together as neatly as possible once the glue has become tacky enough. Any loose headlining or trim can also be stuck in place - but make sure you get an adhesive that's suitable for PVC or vinyl.

Once you've got the seats in a reasonable state of cleanliness and repair, why not consider seat covers? Like the carpets, they're available from specialist firms to suit your car and are a worthwhile buy in view of the protection they give.

If you use your car regularly and you've got the time and inclination it should really be washed every week, either by hand (preferably using a hose pipe) or by taking advantage of the local car-wash if there is one. Whichever method you choose (assuming you wash your car at all!) we don't think we need tell you how to do it - but remember it's never a good idea to just wipe over a dirty car, whether wet or dry, you might as well sandpaper it!

Two or three times a year (even once is better than not at all) a non-abrasive, non-wax emulsion type body polish can be used on the paintwork. We don't know which of the many makes you'll use, so we can only recommend you to follow the maker's instructions closely so that you do see a reward for your efforts. Chrome parts are best cleaned with a special chrome cleaner, ordinary metal polish will attack the finish.

The remainder of this Section describes how to keep your car's bodywork in good condition by dealing with scratches, and more major damage too, as they occur. A number of repair aids and materials are referred to, most of them essential if you're to achieve good results. They should all be available, together with free advice, from good motor accessory shops.

Keeping paintwork up to scratch

With superficial scratches (the sort only other people seem to get) where they don't penetrate down beneath the gel coat (outer skin of the fibreglass), you'll be glad to know that repair can be very simple. Wash the damaged area with clean water and a little washing up liquid to remove any traces of polish. Rinse with plenty of clean water and allow to dry. Apply touch-up paint to the scratch using a fine brush, and continue to build up the paint by several applications, allowing each to dry, until it's level with the surrounding area.

For anyone who's as lazy as we are, the easy alternative to painting over a scratch is to use a 'paint transfer', available in packs to match popular car **87** colours. Prepare the affected area in the same way as for touch-up paint, then simply pick a transfer of a suitable size to cover the scratch completely. Hold the transfer against the area and burnish its backing paper, and if you're doing it right you should find it sticks to the car's paintwork (rather than your hand) and at the same time frees itself from the backing. The patched area can now be polished to blend it in.

When you've got a deep scratch or gouge then it will be necessary to fill the hollow with either cellulose body stopper paste (if its not too deep) or to use one of the proprietary body filler kits. Repairs of this nature are covered below.

Filling and spraying

Many types of body filler are available, but generally speaking those proprietary kits which contain filler paste (or a filler powder and resin liquid) and a separate hardener are best. You'll also need a flexible plastic or nylon applicator (usually supplied) for putting the mixture on with. Mix up a little of the filler on a piece of board or plastic (those plastic margarine tubs are ideal, but do wash out all traces of the contents first!)

Read the instructions carefully and don't mix up too much at one go. You'll find you have to work fairly fast or the mixture will begin to set, especially if you've been a bit generous with the hardener.

Apply the paste to the prepared area more or less to the correct level and contour, but don't try to shape it once it's become tacky or it'll pick up on the applicator. Layers should be built up at intervals until the final level's just proud of the surrounding bodywork.

When the filler's fully hardened, use a Surform plane or coarse file to remove the excess and obtain the final shape. Then follow with progressively finer grades of wet-or-dry abrasive paper starting with coarse, followed by medium, then fine (some manufacturers give 'grit' grades to their wet-or-dry paper – 40 is the coarsest, 400 the finest). Always wrap the paper round a flat block if you're trying to get a flat surface, and keep it wet by rinsing in clean water, or the filler and paint will clog up the abrasive surface.

At this point the doctored area should be surrounded by a ring of bare fibreglass, encircled by a feathered edge of good paintwork. Rinse it with plenty of clean water to get rid of all the paint and filler dust and allow it to dry completely.

If you're happy with the surface you've obtained then you're ready to apply some paint. First spray over the whole area with a light coat of grey primer. This will show up any surface imperfections which may need further treatment, and will also help you get the knack of spraying with an aerosol can before you

Body damage to the rear corner of a Kitten model, showing how the fibreglass material can tear under severe impact. Definitely not a D-I-Y job!

start on the colour coats. Rub down the surface again, and if necessary use a little body stopper, as described for minor scratches to fill any small imperfections. Repeat this spray-and-level procedure until you're satisfied with the finish; then wash down again and allow to dry.

The next stage is to apply the finishing coats, but first of all a word or two about the techniques involved. Paint spraying should be done in a warm, dry, windless, dust-free atmosphere – conditions not very readily available to most of us! You may be able to approach them artificially if you've got a large indoor workshop, but if you have to work outside you'll need to pick the day carefully. If you're working in your garage you may need to 'lay' the dust on the floor by damping it with water.

If the body repair's confined to a small patch, mask off the surrounding area to protect it from paint overspray. Bodywork fittings (chrome strips, door handles and the like) will need to be either masked or removed. If you're masking, use genuine masking tape and plenty of newspaper as necessary. Before starting to spray, shake the aerosol can thoroughly; then experiment on something (an old tin or similar will do - not the neighbour's car!) until you feel you can apply the paint smoothly. At the previous stage this wasn't too important, but now you're trying to get the best possible finish.

First cover the repair area with a thick coat of primer - not as one coat, but built up of several thin ones. When this is dry, using the finest wet-or-dry paper, rub down the surface until it's really smooth. Use plenty of water to keep the surface clean; when it's dry, spray on another primer coat and repeat the procedure.

Now for the top coat. Again the idea's to build up

the paint thickness by several thin coats. Have a test spray first as this is a different aerosol, then commence spraying in the centre of the repair area. Using a circular motion, work gradually outwards towards the edges until the whole of the repair and about two inches of the surrounding original paint is covered. Remove all the masking material 10 to 15 minutes after you've finished spraying.

Now you can start putting away all the bits and pieces because it'll need about two weeks for the paint to harden completely. After this time, using a paint renovator or a very fine cutting paste, blend the edges of the new paint into the original. Finally apply a good quality polish and hopefully you'll have a repair you're proud to own up to.

Holes and splits

As you may know, fibreglass body panels don't rust or dent, but if you hit them hard enough they'll split and maybe a hole will form. Serious damage like that shown in the photographs isn't really a D-I-Y job and is best left to the experts. Minor damage, however, can be tackled by the average owner successfully, provided that the job's done in the correct way.

It's essential to understand a little about how fibreglass behaves and the theory behind it, and to follow the instructions supplied with the repair kit.

Note the following points before starting any repair. Then go on and read the step-by-step instructions accompanying the photographic sequence. Read all the instructions for all the damaged parts of the car before repairing one particular part.

a) The strength and ultimate surface finish of any repair will depend on how thorough you were in preparing the damaged area.

b) If the repair area or materials are damp the strength of the repair will be seriously affected.

c) Don't ruin the job by attempting to smooth the damaged panel before all the resin is hard or cured. Allow plenty of time for this to take place – possibly overnight if the weather's cold. Heat (but not close heat) speeds the curing process. Fibreglass does burn!

d) The true strength of the repair is provided by the fibreglass reinforcement rather than just the resin. Chopped strand matting or cloth must be used with resin to achieve the desired amount of strength. It isn't of any use just to embed layers of fibreglass tissue in resin.

e) Much of the success of any repair depends on the correct mix of the resin. Always follow the instructions given on the manufacturer's packs very closely. They will recommend the

correct proportions of resin to accelerator (hardener). If you're mixing your own resin paste, make sure the proportions of resin and powder are correct. It may be easier to buy a straight paste.

f) When calculating the amount of resin required for a given repair, weigh the cut patches of fibreglass (chopped strand mat) and activate three times this weight of resin.

g) Don't mix more than half a pound of resin at one time. It'll go off before it can be used and you'll end up wasting it.

h) It's very difficult to remove resin and fibre glass from any parts that shouldn't be covered. Remove all such items from the working area and don't wait until the resin is hard before trying to remove it from clothes or any surface. It's a good idea to wear rubber gloves for the job.

i) Finally don't try to rush fibreglass repairs and always give yourself more than enough time for any particular job.

Wing damage

First find the total extent of the damage before attempting to start any preparation or repairs. The best method is to place a high intensity lamp on the inside of the panel to show the true extent of the damage – rather like an X-ray machine. Prepare the damaged area by cleaning off all road dirt, grit and moisture. Failure to carry out this initial preparation will result in poor keying of the new fibreglass.

Always bear in mind the extent of the damage and the quality of the surface finish desired before deciding on a particular method of repair. Cut out the damaged area of the panel so that all the edges are of 'fresh' sound fibreglass laminate. Finish the prepared area for repair by sanding on a rough edge or 'scarf'. File this scarf with its slope on the opposite face to the side from which you are working to enable final keying of the new material.

Temporary moulds can easily be made up from thin aluminium sheeting or a similar material but before fixing it in place, put a layer of cellophane over the total working surface of the mould so that the fibreglass doesn't stick to it (you can use wax polish or polythene sheet as a similar release agent if you wish). Hold the temporary mould on the panel with wide masking tape or self-adhesive tape. Pack any sharp curves with cardboard packing or similar wadding.

Prepare the resin mix (all instructions are always given quite comprehensively on the manufacturer's pack). Using a suitable clean paintbrush, apply a thin coat of neat resin to the inside of the panel under repair and allow this to 'cure' or harden. Having cut **89**

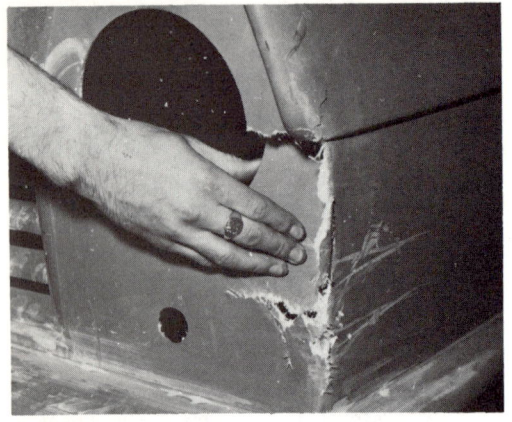
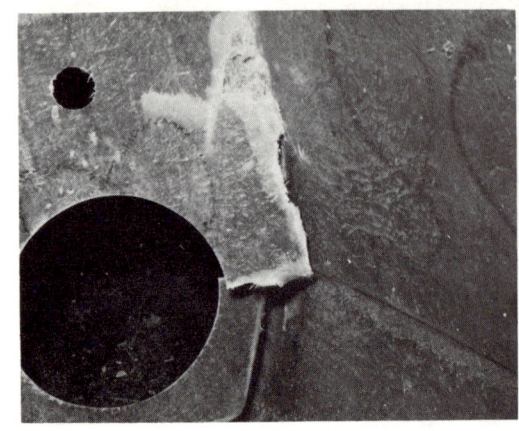
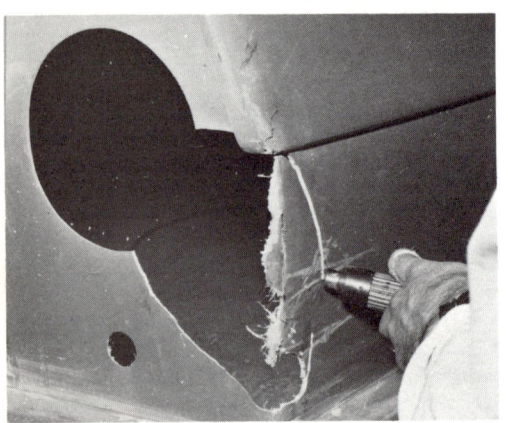

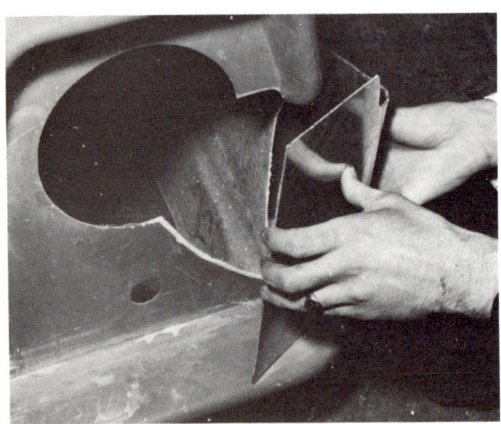

Bodywork repairs ...

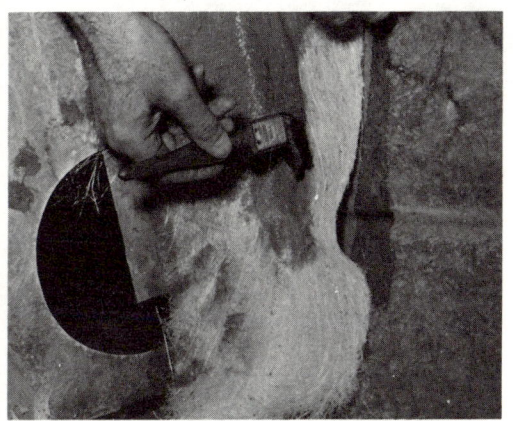

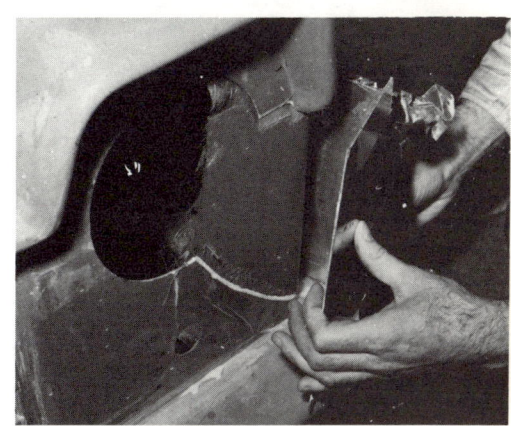

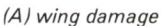

(A) wing damage

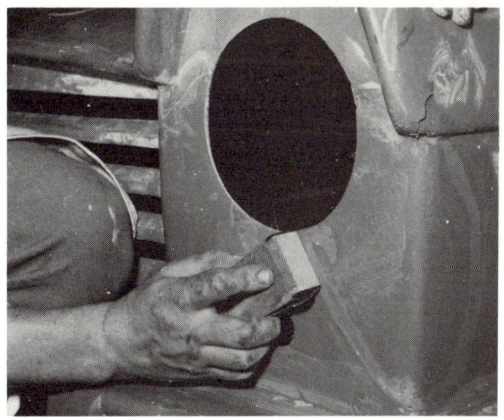

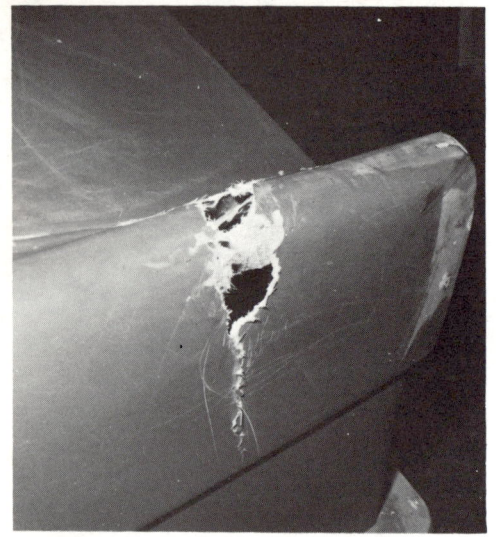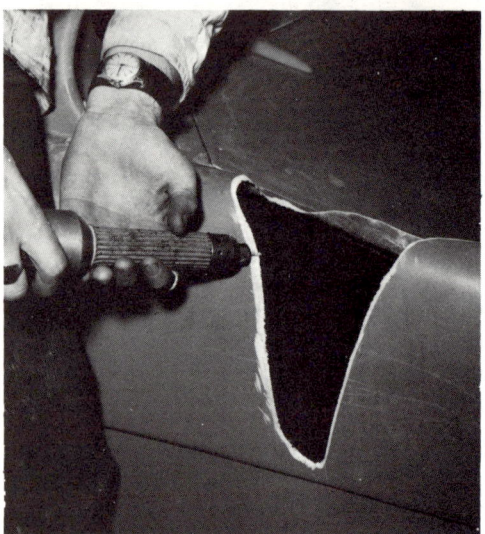

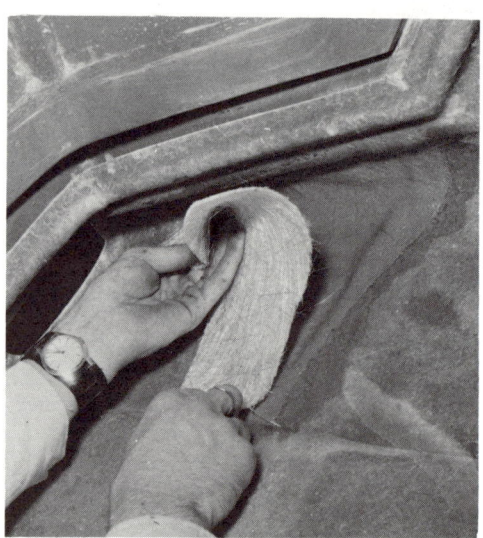

Bodywork repairs – (B) tail damage

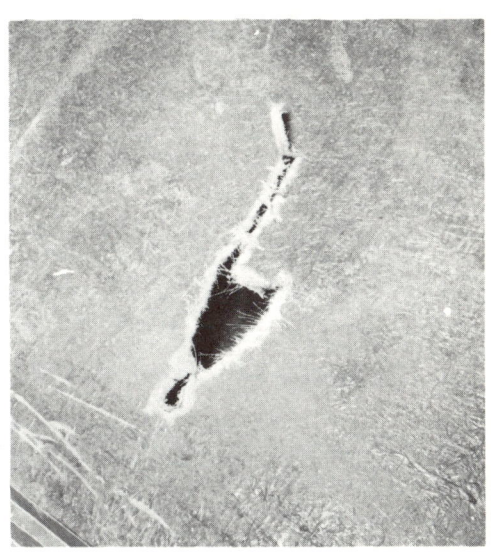

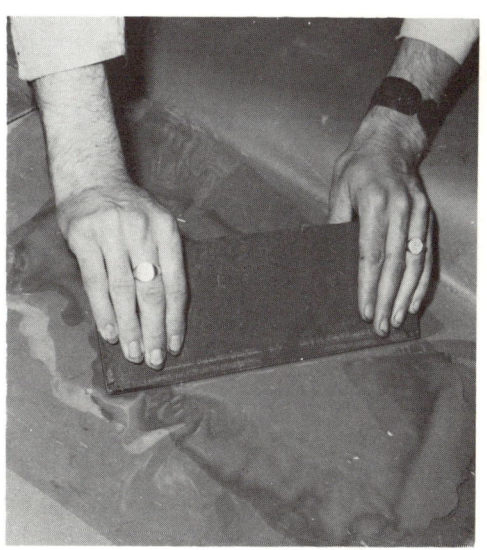

Bodywork repairs – (C) bonnet damage

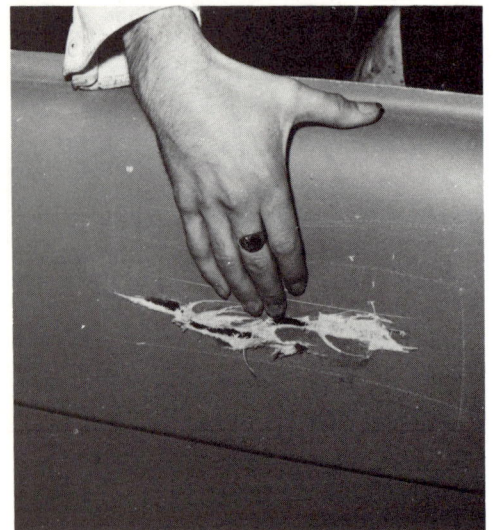
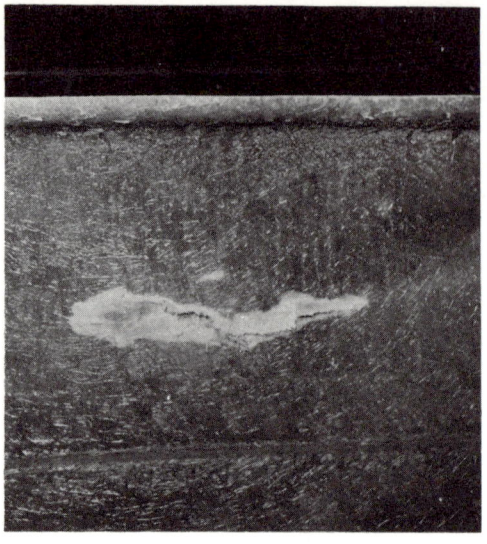
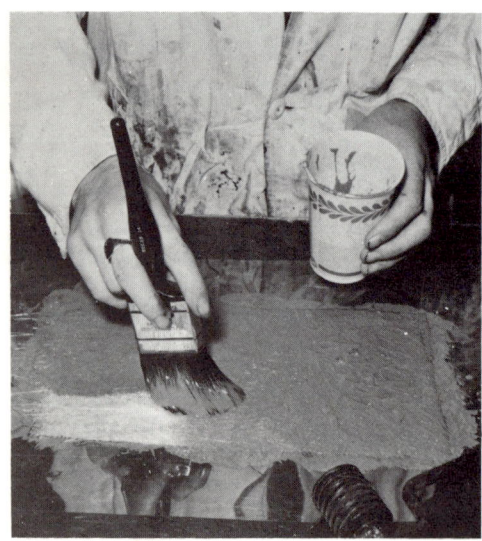

Bodywork repairs – (D) body gash (1)

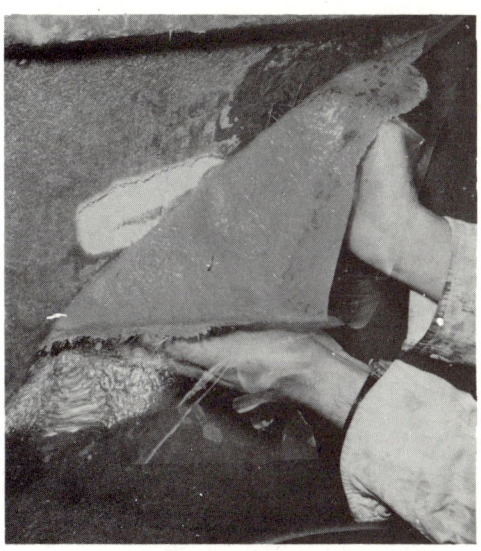
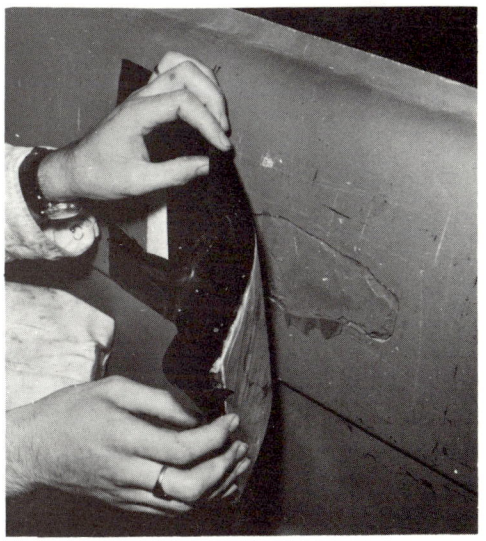
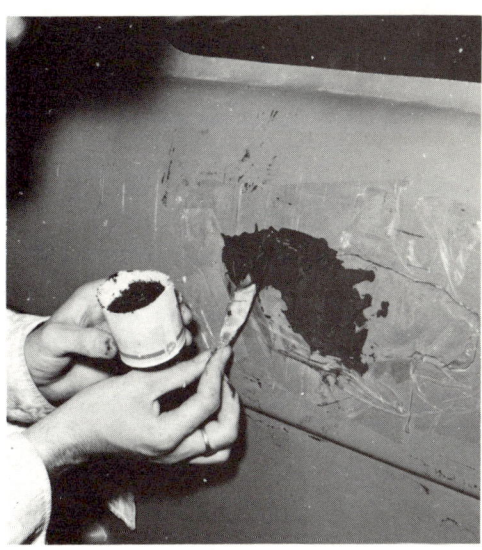

Bodywork repairs – (D) body gash (2)

Bodywork repairs – (E) 'blind' hole

96

up suitably sized pieces of fibreglass matting, paint more resin on to the panel and lay the matting on to it. Stipple in the matting with the brush loaded with more resin. Once the mat is held by the resin it's best to roll the 'new' laminate with a split washer roller. This packs down the matting and forces any trapped air out.

Continue adding matting, stippling and rolling it in, until you reach the desired thickness. Now allow the repair to cure before removing the temporary mould. The release agent should enable you to remove the mould freely (that's if you've applied it correctly and the repair area has fully hardened). Clean up the repaired area with coarse wet-or-dry paper (40 grade), Surform plane and coarse files, but don't be too enthusiastic. Smooth down with finer grades of wet-or-dry paper, and, if necessary, surface imperfections can be filled with body filler as described earlier. Finally the repaired area can be sprayed with primer and finishing coats, again as already described.

Tail damage

Generally speaking the repair procedure is similar to that described for the wing, but because of the more difficult shape involved, detail changes in technique can be used to simplify the task. As before, cut away all the damaged area and 'scarf' the edges in the same way. It's not easy to scarf with an electric drill and rotary sander attachment - it's probably easier to use a coarse file or rasp.

Because of the awkward shape of the rear wing it's best to use adhesive tape such as Sellotape stretched across the damaged area to form a mould. Again paint the inside of the panel with the resin mixture but don't allow it to cure. Having cut the appropriate pieces of matting take the first piece and place it into in a shallow tray along with a small quantity of resin mix. Stipple and roll the matting so that the resin is absorbed into it all over. Now place this piece of matting in position over the damaged area and very carefully stipple and roll it. It is necessary to do the job this way round as the mould isn't very rigid. Once the first layer has been positioned and allowed to cure apply the next layers in the normal manner directly on to the repair area.

Bonnet damage

In the photograph sequence the damage appears to be slight from the outside, but from the inside it can be seen that it's much more extensive. Consequently a much larger hole must be cut than was first envisaged to reach sound laminate.

The mould must be slightly curved to match the bonnet contour; it can be placed inside the bonnet and temporarily secured by adhesive tape, but don't forget the release agent. Apply resin and matting as described previously, taking care to stipple and roll each piece in position. Because a fine finish is required on the outside of the flat surface of the bonnet, apply a final coat of resin on top of all the other work.

Place on top of this a piece of Cellophane and 'squeeze' it flat allowing the surface of the Cellophane to smooth off the surface of the resin. Remove the Cellophane when this resin has cured, and then finally smooth off and paint in the normal manner.

Body gashes

If the bodywork is scratched badly, even if the surface doesn't appear to be badly broken, it's still essential to replace any lost strength and to regain the smooth outer surface of that panel. It's probable that the damage will extend further than just the 'external' scratch itself. Check from inside the panel to see the extent of the damage.

Cut out the damaged section, as previously described and cut the scarf to the outside as the repair should be made from the inside. On flat surfaces which are almost vertical e.g. side of the front wing, it's easier to 'wet-out' the fibreglass matting in a tin tray first. Lay out a piece of Cellophane which is larger than the piece of matting and paint it with resin. Place the matting on this resin and stipple it. Now roll it out, still in the tray, with a split washer roller to push out any air bubbles.

Paint the inside of the panel with some resin, having placed a temporary mould on the outer side fixed with adhesive tape and painted with release agent. Offer up the Cellophane sheet and soaked fibreglass matting, hold it in position and allow it to cure. When the repair material has cured, remove the mould and Cellophane sheet and complete the repair in the usual manner.

'Blind' panels

There may be odd occasions when it's not possible to reach both sides of the damaged panel. This does make the repair more difficult but by no means impossible. Cut out the damaged area as described previously, but from the outside, and try to do this to the shape of a rectangle, clean and neat. Now prepare an appreciably larger rectangle of fibreglass mat in a flat tin tray with resin, again as previously described, and allow to cure.

Once this panel has cured, push strands of wire through this moulded sheet and use them as a holder. Paint more resin on this moulded sheet and add small pieces of rough mat to it. Pass this prepared panel carefully through the rectangular hole cut out in the body and hold onto the panel with the wire holder.

The prepared panel must now be held firmly in **97**

position against the damaged area. The easiest method is to tie a piece of strong string to the wire holders and to secure the other end of the string to a convenient object, such as a hook in the garage wall. With the string still in position, apply a few pieces of matting with resin to the edges of the repair area so that the prepared panel will be retained in position.

Allow the surface to cure and then carefully remove the string and wire holders. Fill the damaged patch with more resin and rough mat until it's flush with the original surface. Finally finish off with neat resin, place a piece of Cellophane over the top and squeeze flat. This will provide the desired surface on which to start the final smoothing, flatting and painting. Use regular body filler to fill any irregularities as previously described.

Adding 'Pinstripes'

There are various kinds of self-adhesive body decor available for customising your car, although some Reliant models already have side stripes. Perhaps the neatest and most suitable of the 'add on' variety are Pinstripes, and we've included these here as they may appeal to the owner who wants a cheap and simple way to improve the appearance of his or her car. They are adhesive tapes which come in different widths and colours and as single or multi-stripes, with a backing paper which is peeled off as the stripe is applied.

When applying any of these self-adhesive tapes, first make sure that the paintwork's clean by washing with warm water and a car shampoo or liquid detergent. You can now apply the tape, but follow the directions carefully. Smooth it down with a clean rag and, if necessary, prick out any small air bubbles with a pin. Try not to stretch the stripes as you put them on because they'll shrink slightly anyway; and wrap the ends round the panels so that they don't pull away at the edges.

The Personal Touch

A vast multitude of accessories is available these days to enable you to transform even the most basic Reliant model into the 'luxury' class. Go into the average accessory shop and you're faced with such a line-up of 'special offers' that if you're not careful you'll be broke before you are half-way round this Aladdin's Cave of motoring paraphernalia, so first sort out your most immediate needs and give them priority.

Reliant market a wide range of accessories that are tailor-made to fit your Reliant model, and of course you'll get expert fitting advice from your Reliant dealer. If the item you want isn't in the Reliant range, or a similar product's more competitively priced from a general accessory shop, make sure firstly that it's suitable for your model, and secondly that you're able, and have the tools required, to install it. Many accessory packs today list the car models that they'll fit but check with the supplier before buying.

All good products will be supplied with general instructions which may or may not require minor modifications to suit your Reliant. If you're buying secondhand, of course, you may get no instructions at all. The guidelines given here are in no way intended to replace the manufacturer's instructions and if you're in doubt about fitting a particular item they're the people to refer to.

We'd need several volumes to discuss all the various kinds of things you might conceivably buy for your car, and those that we've managed to mention can't be gone into in great detail in a book like this. Some time spent browsing around a good motor accessory shop will reveal more than we can here, but nevertheless we hope the suggestions given may be useful.

Note: always disconnect the battery before commencing any work involving the electrical system. Remember too that most electrical items have to be earthed in some way or other, and the Reliant is made from fibre glass which is a non-conducting material. It's for this reason that separate earth wires must be run to a convenient earthing point on the vehicle chassis for each electrical component.

Auxiliary instruments

It would be possible to write a complete book on auxiliary instruments and how to fit them but, as with other things, you'll normally get pretty good instructions when you buy them. Because there are so many instruments available, we're only going to consider ammeters, battery condition indicators, clocks, oil pressure gauges, tachometers and vacuum gauges.

First of all, even before you've decided what instruments you're going to fit, you've got to think where to fit them. The dash panels of some Reliant models are pretty full before you start, so you may have to resort to fitting brackets and small extra panels. Some instruments such as tachometers can be pod types, which are attached to the top of the dash panel. Another answer may be to modify the **99**

Some of the supplementary instruments and other accessories available from Smiths Industries

central console (where fitted) to accommodate extra instruments or switches.

Sooner or later you're going to have to start drilling some holes somewhere, but this needn't cause any real headaches if it's approached in the right way. Make sure that there's nothing behind the panel before you even consider drilling a hole, and that there's enough room to fit the instrument, switch or whatever in the space chosen. Any hole which will have a cable or capillary running through it must have a plastic or rubber grommet to prevent the possibility of any sharp edges chafing through; these grommets can be obtained from D-I-Y accessory or car electrical shops.

Ammeter

The ammeter must be connected in such a way that it registers all the current supplied to, or drawn from, the battery except for the starting circuit. On models fitted with an alternator you'll need an instrument that reads to plus and minus 40 amps, while for the earlier models fitted with a dynamo, an ammeter with a reading of plus and minus 30 amps is acceptable.

It's essential that the wiring's correct and that a heavy gauge wire is used, so follow the instructions carefully, or get expert advice before you start. If, after the ammeter's connected, it's found to be indicating in the reverse sense, simply change over the connections on the back of the instrument.

Battery condition indicator

The battery condition indicator's simply a voltmeter, and as such must be connected to a good earth point on the chassis and to any suitable connection which is live when the ignition's switched on. For convenience, this could be the fuse for the direction indicators and windscreen wiper circuits. You won't need heavy cables for the battery condition indicator - 14/0.30(14/.012) should be OK but make

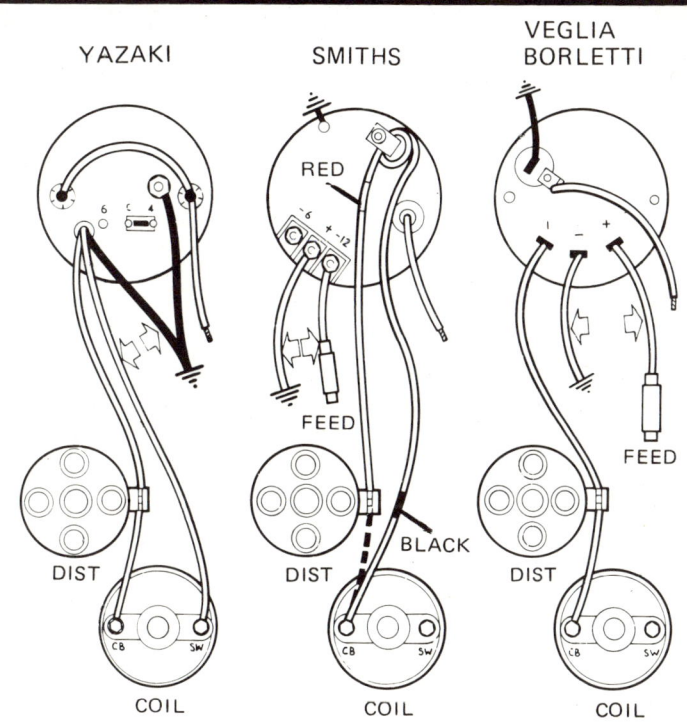

Connections for three popular tachometers

Yazaki: Negative earth shown – reverse arrowed wires to change polarity.
Smiths: Positive earth shown – the dotted connection must be removed when the tachometer is fitted.
                Reverse arrowed wires to change polarity.
Veglia Borletti: Negative earth shown – reverse arrowed wires to change polarity.

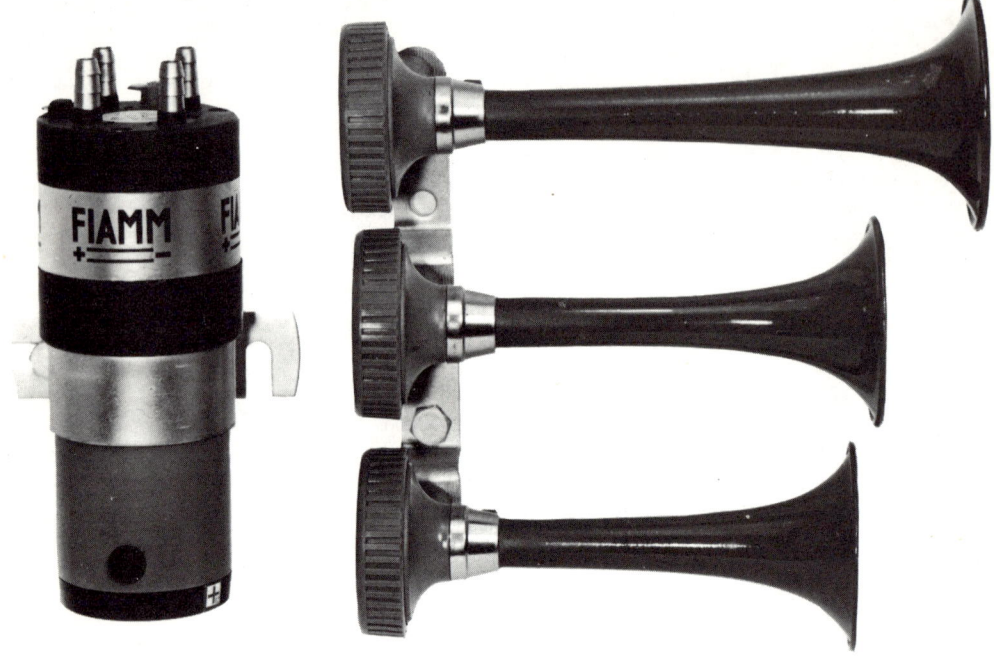

Fiamm 'Trio' air horns

sure that the earth polarity's correct.

Clock

Clocks come in many forms, but most types contain semi-conductors. If this means nothing to you, remember that while it ensures a negligible load on the battery it does mean that the polarity (positive/negative earth connections) is critical if you don't want to cause permanent damage, so watch the maker's instructions here. Connections are much the same as for the battery condition indicator except that you don't want the clock to stop when the ignition's switched off. Therefore a suitable connecting point could be the fuse for the horn and lighting system.

Tachometer

The tachometer (rev counter) is the one instrument that's available in larger sizes than the others (80 mm istead of 52 mm, although the smaller size can be obtained). Most are positive or negative earth, but you must connect them up correctly. In case you should pick up a secondhand one, connections for the most common types are shown in the illustrations. Note that with the Smiths type, the distributor to coil LT lead is remved; also note the sleeve colours on the main white lead. Use a 14/0.30 (14/.012) cable size.

Oil pressure gauge

If you really care about your engine then this is a 'must'. The oil pressure warning light will only inform you that something's wrong when it's possibly too late or too inconvenient to do anything about it. The pressure gauge indicates the engine oil pressure, which in turn tells you the basic condition of your engine; any sudden or gradual decline in pressure can be noted and the fault rectified before the situation's serious. Two types of gauge are available: the mechanical type with a small-bore copper or nylon tube to the gauge from the engine, and the electrical type in which an electrical sensing device transmits a varying voltage to the gauge. With either type a 'T' piece will be required to enable it to be connected into the existing oil pressure warning light socket whilst still retaining the warning light.

Warning devices

Air horns

Air horns are marketed by several companies as a D-I-Y installation kit comprising the horns themselves, a compressor unit, a relay, plastic piping and electric cable. What you've obviously got to do is to mount the horns reasonably near the compressor, and the compressor reasonably near the relay, or the connections just won't reach. It's normal for the manufacturers to specify a certain way up for the compressor to be mounted, but there shouldn't be any other problems.

You'll need to make sure that the electrical connections are as per the maker's instructions for the relay and compressor, and decide whether you want to use the air horns in conjunction with, or in place of, the original car horn. If you have to connect into existing wiring, make sure the connections are well made and if these involve soldering, don't forget to insulate any soldered joints.

Hazard warning

It's to be hoped that you'll never break down on a busy road or in an awkward spot, but if it does happen it's reassuring to have a hazard warning system fitted. This is a device which enables all four direction indicator lamps to flash simultaneously to warn other vehicles that you're stationary and to help them spot you in poor visibility – not (despite frequent use for the purpose) to indicate that you've parked on double yellow lines to pop into the tobacconists'! Full instructions are supplied with these kits, but wiring can be tricky as a number of connections have to be made into existing circuits.

KL's 'Jeenay' child safety seat

Child safety seats and harnesses

Much has been said in recent years about the use of seat belts for front seat passengers, and more recently there's been an increasing interest in the various special rear seats and harnesses now available, for young children. It's very difficult to give any precise instructions for fitting these, because there are so many types around, but what you must be careful about is ensuring that you buy a BSI-approved type.

Most types have a pair of straps at the lower edge which need to be attached to the rear seat pan at the back of the squab, and a further pair of straps that fit over the back of the car seat for attachment to the rear parcel shelf (or the floor or wheel arch with estate cars). Take very careful note of the manufacturers' instructions; they require the anchorages to be a certain distance apart, and may also require reinforcing plates to be used.

Before starting to drill holes for the mountings, make sure that the underside or rear of the panel's clear of obstructions, pipes or any other components. It may also be possible to utilise existing tapped fitting points. If you're in doubt, get in touch with the seat or harness manufacturers - they'll be only too pleased to give advice.

Lamps

When auxiliary lamps are fitted, not only must you fit them in a suitable place on the car, but that place must also meet certain legal requirements. Where these apply we've attempted to give some guide lines.

In addition to the actual lights themselves, we have to think of the switches (not normally difficult because many small switch panels are available, or you may already have a console which will take them, or you can simply drill a hole in a suitable spot on the dashboard), fusing, cable sizes, and whether relays are necessary.

Spot and fog lamps

It's illegal to mount these with their centres *more than* 3ft 6 in (1067mm) above the ground. Any lamps that are mounted with their centres *less than* 2 ft (610 mm) above the ground may only be used *in conjunction with* headlamps. The lamps must always be mounted and used in pairs (two fog, two spot or one of each) if they're to be used independently of the headlamps. Their inner edges must be *not less than* 13.8 in (350 mm) apart and their outer edges must be *within* 15.75 in (400 mm) of the edge of the car. If they're used as spotlamps, they must conform to the normal anti-dazzle requirements by wiring them via the dipswitch or by pointing them slightly downwards.

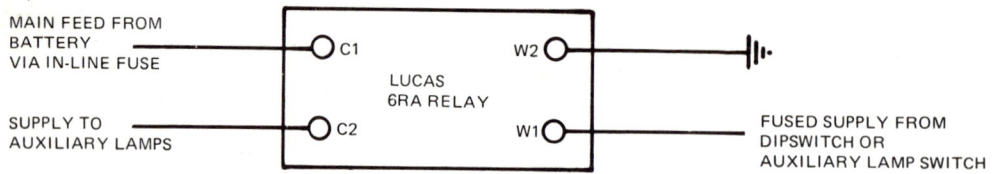

Typical connections for auxiliary lamps using a relay

Choose the lamps carefully, and if possible match the lamp styles. There are many good types on sale, so if you're not sure what you want seek some advice.

To prevent overload of the switch or wiring, a relay should be used (Lucas 6RA type, part no. 33213, is suitable - see illustration). This is connected through the switch from the existing headlamp circuit to one of the relay 'coil' terminals, the other going to a good earth point. The lamp wires then go to one of the relay 'contact' terminals, with the other terminal going either to the battery or the battery terminal on the starter solenoid via an in-line fuse. The fuse rating will depend on the lamp manufacturer's recommendations, but will probably be about 20 amps for both lamps. A good place to mount the relay is fairly near the starter solenoid and battery, to reduce the cable runs to a minimum.

Reversing lamps

Reversing lamps come in many shapes and sizes but the flush-fitting type are preferable. These lamps can be purchased as a complete kit comprising lamps, wire and switch. Don't forget that if you're not using a switch which is fitted with an illuminated warning light you'll have to wire up a separate warning light wired in parallel with the reverse lamp. An in-line fuse will be needed, probably about 10 amps rating, but it will depend on the actual lamp(s) fitted.

Rear fog lights

These can be mounted in much the same way as reversing lamps, although bumper-mounted types tend to be popular. For wiring, the same sort of instructions apply as for reversing lights (in fact some types serve a dual purpose in having a clear lens for reversing and a red snap on lens for the fog light).

Anti-theft devices

There are three main categories of car thieves - those people who want your car either as a complete item or for the major mechanical and body parts; those who are out for a joy-ride; and those who merely want the contents. With any type of thief it makes sense to do what you can to deter someone from wanting to get in; don't leave valuables lying about, don't leave the car unlocked and, if it's parked at home, put it in a locked garage if possible. But if a car thief decides he does want your car, statistically he's got a pretty good chance of getting it!

All Kitten models have a steering column lock which is a very effective protection against a car being driven away, but it still makes sense to have a good burglar alarm fitted. Many types are available, and many of these are wired into door courtesy light switches or hidden switches beneath seats. Other types are wired into the horn circuit, but separate horns and bells are available; the more unconventional it is (whilst still being reliable) the better. Don't put hidden switches in the first place you think of - it might be the first place the thief thinks of too!

Some anti-theft devices are actuated by the movement caused by somebody trying to get into the car (and occasionally by an innocent passer-by). Some not only sound alarms, but also earth the ignition circuit; other devices simply lock together the steering wheel and brake pedal. Have a look around the accessory shops and see what suits your car, your pocket and the amount of protection required.

Radios and tape players

A radio or tape player's an expensive item to buy, and will only give its best performance if fitted properly. It's useless to expect concert hall performance from a unit that's suspended from the

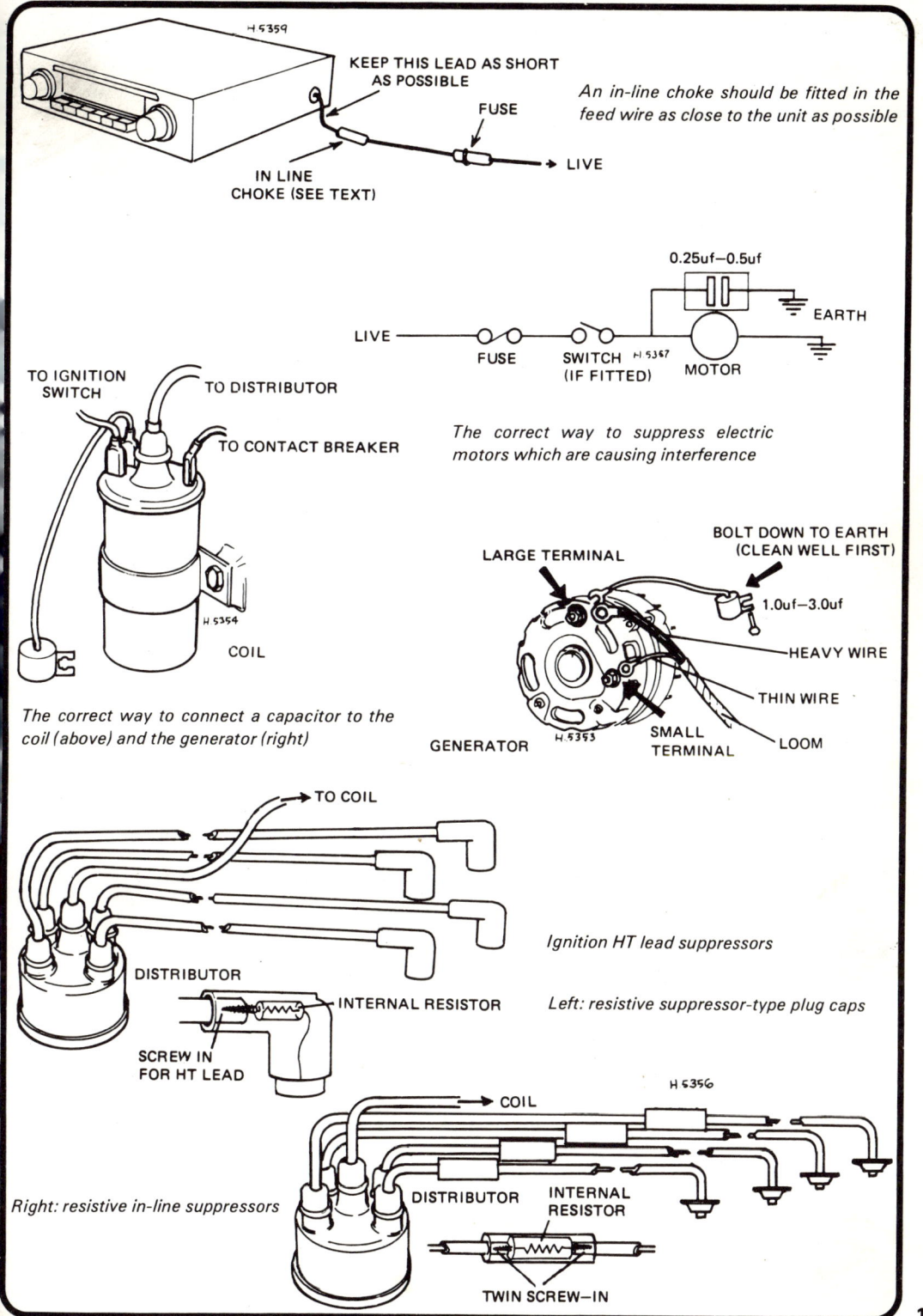

H 5359

KEEP THIS LEAD AS SHORT
AS POSSIBLE

FUSE

*An in-line choke should be fitted in the
feed wire as close to the unit as possible*

IN LINE
CHOKE (SEE TEXT)

LIVE

0.25uf–0.5uf

LIVE

FUSE

SWITCH
(IF FITTED)

H 5367

MOTOR

EARTH

*The correct way to suppress electric
motors which are causing interference*

TO IGNITION
SWITCH

TO DISTRIBUTOR

TO CONTACT BREAKER

H 5354

COIL

BOLT DOWN TO EARTH
(CLEAN WELL FIRST)

1.0uf–3.0uf

LARGE TERMINAL

HEAVY WIRE

THIN WIRE

LOOM

GENERATOR

H 5353

SMALL
TERMINAL

*The correct way to connect a capacitor to the
coil (above) and the generator (right)*

TO COIL

DISTRIBUTOR

INTERNAL RESISTOR

SCREW IN
FOR HT LEAD

Ignition HT lead suppressors

Left: resistive suppressor-type plug caps

H 5356

COIL

DISTRIBUTOR

INTERNAL
RESISTOR

Right: resistive in-line suppressors

TWIN SCREW–IN

dash panel by string with its speaker(s) resting on the back seat or parcel shelf! If you don't want to do the installation yourself, there are many in-car entertainment specialists who can do the fitting for you.

Make sure the unit purchased is of the same polarity as the car, or that units with adjustable polarity are correctly set before commencing installation.

It's difficult to give specific information about fitting, as final positioning of the radio/tape player, speakers and aerial is entirely a matter of your own personal preference. However, the following paragraphs give guidelines to follow, relevant to all installations.

Radios

Most radios are a standardised size of 7 inches wide by 2 inches deep; this ensures that they'll fit into the radio aperture provided in many cars.

The following points should be borne in mind before deciding exactly where to fit the unit:

a) It should be in easy reach of the driver wearing a seat belt.

b) It shouldn't be mounted close to an electric tachometer, the ignition switch and its wiring, or the flasher unit and associated wiring.

c) It should be mounted within reach of the aerial lead (you can use an extension cable if necessary) and in such a place that the aerial lead won't have to be routed near the components detailed in (b).

d) It shouldn't be positioned in a place where it might cause injury to the car occupants in an accident; for instance, under the dash panel above the driver's or passenger's legs.

e) It should be fitted really securely.

The type of aerial used, and where you're going to fit it, is a matter of personal preference. In general the taller the aerial, the better the reception but there are limits to what's practicable. If you can, fit a fully retractable type - it saves an awful lot of problems with vandals and car wash equipment. When choosing a suitable spot for the aerial, remember the following points:

a) The aerial lead should be as short as possible.

b) The aerial should be mounted as far away from the distributor and HT leads as possible.

c) The part of the aerial which protrudes beneath the mounting point mustn't foul the roadwheels, or anything else.

d) If possible the aerial should be positioned so that the lead doesn't have to be routed

through the engine compartment.

e) The aerial should be mounted at a more-or-less vertical angle.

Radio interference suppression

Books have been written on the subject, so we're not going to be able to tell you a lot in this small space. To reduce the possibility of your radio picking up unwanted interference, an in-line choke should be fitted in the feed wire and the set itself must be earthed really securely. The next step is to start connecting capacitors to reduce the amount of interference being generated by the different circuits of the car's electrics.

The accompanying illustrations show the various interference sources and give capacitor values for the suppressors. When it comes to the ignition HT leads, there are resistors which can either be suppressor type plug caps or in-line suppressors; if you're already using resistive HT leads (those with carbon fibre filling), they're already doing the job for you.

Tape players

Fitting procedures for both cartridge and cassette tape players are the same and in general the same rules apply as when fitting a radio. Tape players aren't usually prone to electrical interference like radios (although it can occur) so positioning isn't so critical. If possible the player should be mounted on an even keel. Also it must be possible for a driver wearing a seat belt to reach the unit in order to change or turn over tapes.

Visibility aids

Mirrors

Recent EEC legislation has done wonders for the looks of exterior mirrors. In addition to being functional, they now must have no projections to catch clothing or other vehicles and must fold flat when struck. The result is a new wave of products in all shapes and sizes some of which can be sprayed to match the existing car finish. There has also been a marked swing recently from wing mirrors to the door-mounted kind, and these are available, to fit either side of the car.

Choose mirrors which you think will suit the car's styling and, having got them, select the mounting point carefully. You'll get a good idea of the best place by simply looking at other cars, but get someone to hold the mirror while you sit in the driving seat just to make sure you can see all you need to.

Mark the position on the wing or door, and if you're fitting two mirrors do likewise on the other to make sure that they're both in the same position. Check the hole size needed and, if you can, select a

MAG 'European' door mirror

drill this size, plus a smaller one to make a pilot hole. If you haven't got the larger drill required for most wing mirrors, you'll have to drill several small holes and file them out to the correct size.

Don't forget to remove any burrs from the hole afterwards; fit the mirror following the manufacturer's instructions, then angle it as necessary to get the best rear view.

Rear window demisters

At one time, if your car wasn't fitted with a heated rear window as standard equipment (and only the expensive models were) about the only remedy was a stick-on clear panel designed to act a bit like double glazing. They didn't usually work very well and frequently came unstuck too. Now they've been more or less superseded by the element type of stick-on demister. These act more like the genuine article, consisting of a metal foil element which is peeled off a backing sheet and stuck on the inside surface of the rear window glass. It has to be wired up to the electrical system, of course, via a suitable fuse and switch, using sufficiently heavy cable and preferably incorporating a warning lamp as it will take quite a large current and shouldn't be left on inadvertently. Make sure the glass is thoroughly clean before fitting. The great thing about these devices is that they do

work and are very moderately priced.

Headlamp conversions

Still on the subject of better visibility, if your problem's seeing in the dark then you might well consider uprating your headlamps. A number of conversions are available for the standard round and rectangular type of headlamps. Fitting usually involves a direct replacement with the old ones and no wiring alterations are required. Headlamp unit removal and fitting instructions are given in *In an Emergency*.

Comfort

Longer journeys can be much more pleasant if your car's comfortable to drive, and just a couple of suggestions on this theme may be welcome.

Sound reducing kits

There are few mass-produced cars in which the noise level, particularly at motorway speeds, is all that could be desired. For economy reasons most manufacturers put only a certain amount of underfelt and sound-deadening material into their cars, and a further improvement can usually be made by fitting one of the proprietary kits. These are usually tailored to fit individual models and consist of sections of felt-like material which are glued in place under carpets, inside hollow sections, boot lid etc, in accordance with instructions . The material can also be bought in rolls for D-I-Y cutting, using the carpets etc as templates.

Seats

If your car seats are showing signs of old age (and just fitting new covers won't disguise the sagging when you sit in them) then you can of course have them rebuilt by an upholstery specialist. On the other hand, if you feel that the seats in the Reliant models aren't the most comfortable ever made, you could think about replacing at least thedriver's seat with one of the special bucket types available. To look at these you'll have to find an accessory shop stocking the more motor sport orientated kind of goods.

Miscellaneous

Electronic ignition

Such systems are many and varied and widely advertised. The makers claim easier starting, better performance and lower fuel consumption as the main advantages, and on the whole these claims are substantiated in practice. However, before buying one of the available kits we suggest you stop and reflect whether your mileage and type of driving makes the expenditure worthwhile. Get other advice, preferably from someone who's fitted such a system to his own car. Consider too whether you're capable of installing it yourself, otherwise you'll have to pay for fitting as well.

There are several types of electronic ignition; some retain the conventional contact-breakers in the car's distributor while others replace this by a magnetic triggering device. Even where the contact points are retained they're no longer likely to burn and therefore shouldn't need replacing so frequently but this doesn't in itself amount to much of a saving.

Roof racks

Many an owner has to resort to a luggage rack from time to time, even if it's only for family holidays.

The types available are varied, but they normally rely on clips attached to the water drain channel above the doors. If you're buying, select a size that suits your requirements, making sure that it's not too wide for the roof!

When fitting the roof rack, position it squarely on the roof, preferably towards the front rather than the rear. After it's loaded, by the way, recheck the tension of the attachment bracket screws.

Don't keep the roof rack on when it's not needed; it offers too much wind resistance and creates a surprising amount of noise (see *Save It!*)

Dog/luggage guards

Owners of estate car versions of the Robin and Kitten who either own a dog or carry large loads in the rear of the vehicle will no doubt find one of these tubular barriers beneficial. They're normally adjustable telescopically, both for height and width, and are fitted by clamping between roof and load deck immediately behind the rear seat to keep dog, luggage or whatever in its rightful place and possibly prevent injury to the front seat occupants in an emergency stop.

Mudflaps

You're probably aware that mudflaps can be fitted to both the front (Kitten) and rear wheel arches of your Reliant. These will not only protect your car's underside and paintwork from flying stones, but will also earn the thanks of following drivers owing to the reduction in spray during wet weather. Fitting's straightforward and is usually by means of clamping brackets or self tapping screws.

Specialist fitments

We've now covered a lot of main items likely to interest the average owner from the D-I-Y fitting angle. Such things as towbars, and sunshine or vinyl roofs, while practical or desirable, are beyond the scope of this Handbook and of the average car owner. We therefore recommend that for any major accessory of this kind you consult the appropriate specialist who'll be able to give an initial estimate of the cost as well as carrying out the work properly and safely.

Troubleshooting

We've gone to great lengths in this Handbook to provide as much information on your car as we think you'll need for satisfactory running and D-I-Y servicing. Hopefully, you won't need to use this Section but there's always a possibility (rather than a probability!) that something will go wrong, and by reference to the charts which follow you should be able to pinpoint the trouble even if you can't actually fix it yourself.

The charts are broken down into the main systems of the car and, where there's a fairly straightforward remedy — the sort you can tackle yourself — **bold type** is used to highlight it. Further information on that particular item will normally be found elsewhere in the Handbook; look up the component or system in the index to find the correct page. In some cases a reference number will be found (e.g. T1/1) and by looking up this number in the accompanying Cross-reference Table, you'll find more information on that particular fault. **109**

TROUBLESHOOTER 1:

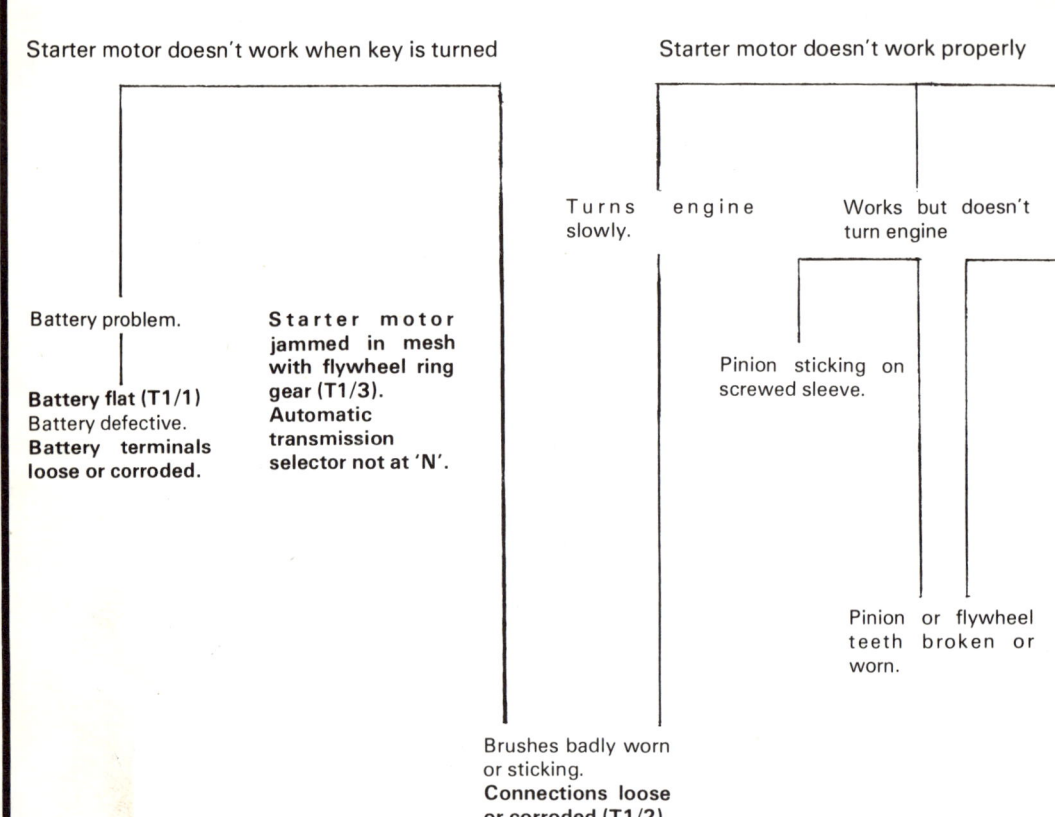

Starter motor doesn't work when key is turned

Battery problem.

Battery flat (T1/1)
Battery defective.
Battery terminals loose or corroded.

Starter motor jammed in mesh with flywheel ring gear (T1/3).
Automatic transmission selector not at 'N'.

Brushes badly worn or sticking.
Connections loose or corroded (T1/2).
Internal fault in motor or solenoid.

Starter motor doesn't work properly

Turns engine slowly.

Works but doesn't turn engine

Pinion sticking on screwed sleeve.

Pinion or flywheel teeth broken or worn.

ENGINE — STARTING

Starter motor turns engine normally but engine won't start

Works noisily or harshly.

Starter main spring broken.
Retaining bolts loose (T1/7).

Ignition problem.

Spark plug lead(s) loose, disconnected, or damp (T1/4).
Spark plugs dirty, cracked or incorrectly gapped.
Distributor or coil cap cracked or HT lead loose.
Worn distributor cap electrodes.
Coil or condenser faulty (T1/5).
Contact breaker points dirty or incorrectly set.
Ignition timing incorrect.

Fuel problem.

Fuel pump faulty, or filter blocked (T1/6).
Leak in fuel pump or fuel lines.
Carburettor float chamber fuel level(s) incorrect.
Carburettor incorrectly adjusted.
Choke not operating correctly.

Other causes

Air cleaner blocked.
Valve clearances incorrect.
Inlet manifold or gasket or carburettor gasket leaking.

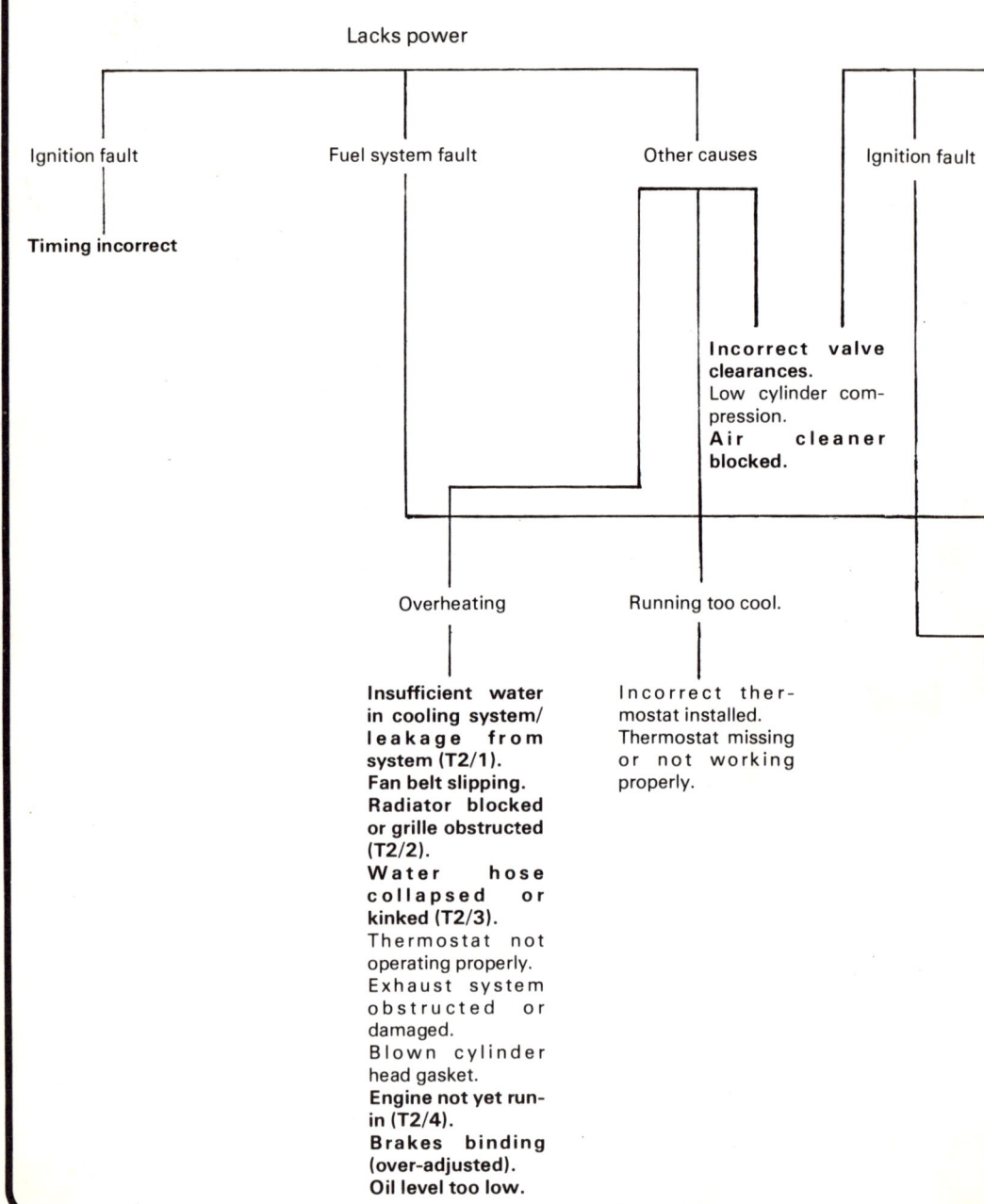

Lacks power

Ignition fault

Fuel system fault

Other causes

Ignition fault

Timing incorrect

Incorrect valve clearances.
Low cylinder compression.
Air cleaner blocked.

Overheating

Running too cool.

Insufficient water in cooling system/ leakage from system (T2/1). Fan belt slipping. Radiator blocked or grille obstructed (T2/2). Water hose collapsed or kinked (T2/3). Thermostat not operating properly. Exhaust system obstructed or damaged. Blown cylinder head gasket. **Engine not yet run-in (T2/4). Brakes binding (over-adjusted). Oil level too low.**

Incorrect thermostat installed. Thermostat missing or not working properly.

ENGINE — RUNNING

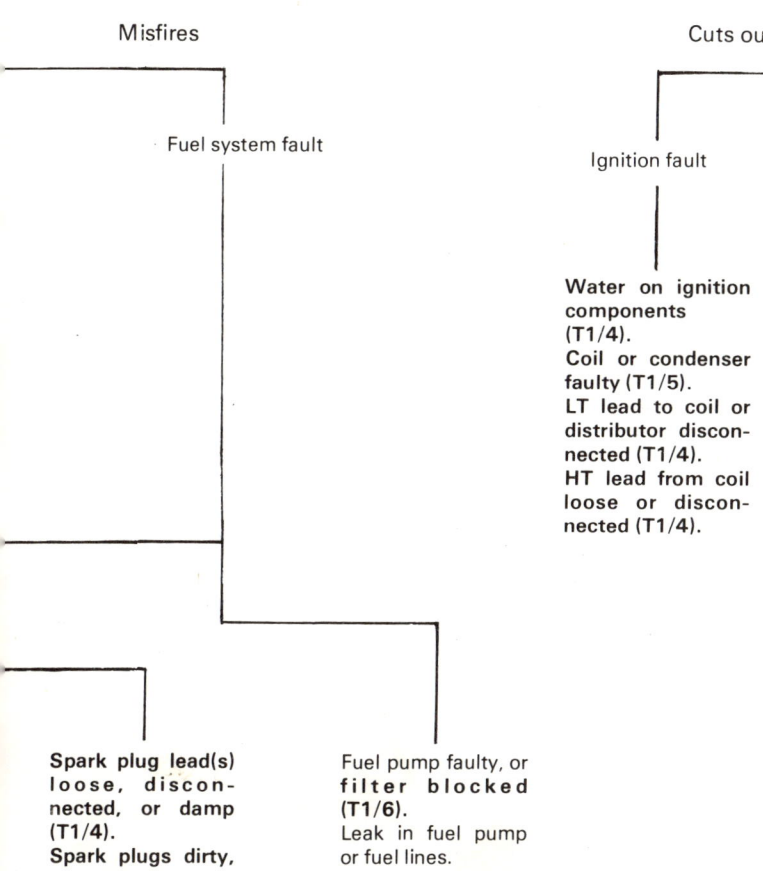

Misfires

Fuel system fault

Cuts out unexpectedly

Ignition fault

Fuel system fault

Water on ignition components (T1/4).
Coil or condenser faulty (T1/5).
LT lead to coil or distributor disconnected (T1/4).
HT lead from coil loose or disconnected (T1/4).

Tank empty.
Fuel pump faulty or filter blocked (T1/6).
Fuel line broken, leaking or blocked.

Spark plug lead(s) loose, disconnected, or damp (T1/4).
Spark plugs dirty, cracked or incorrectly gapped.
Distributor or coil cap damp, cracked or HT lead loose.
Worn distributor cap electrodes.
Coil or condenser faulty (T1/5).
Contact breaker points dirty or incorrectly set.
Ignition timing incorrect.

Fuel pump faulty, or filter blocked (T1/6).
Leak in fuel pump or fuel lines.
Carburettor jet blocked.
Carburettor float chamber fuel lines incorrect.
Carburettor incorrectly adjusted.
Choke not operating correctly.

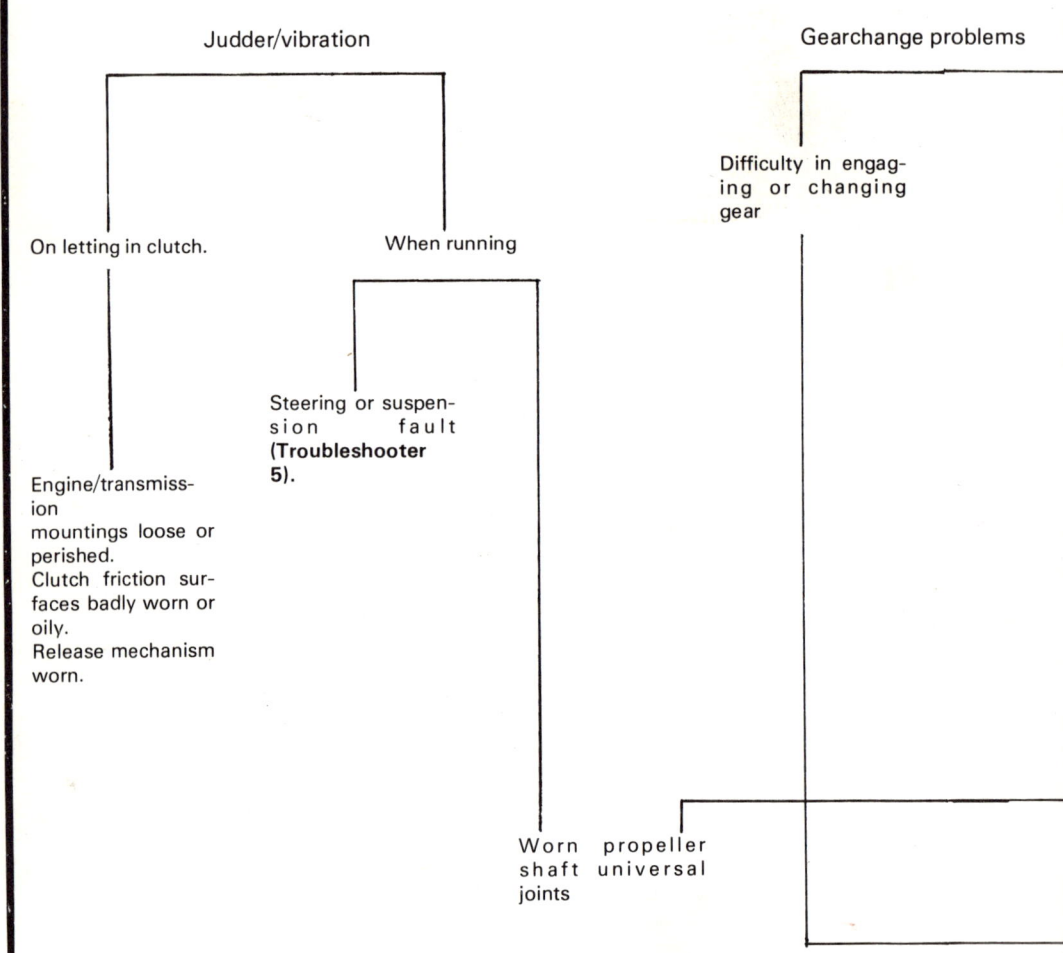

Judder/vibration

On letting in clutch.

When running

Steering or suspen-
sion   fault
**(Troubleshooter
5).**

Engine/transmiss-
ion
mountings loose or
perished.
Clutch friction sur-
faces badly worn or
oily.
Release mechanism
worn.

Worn   propeller
shaft universal
joints

Gearchange problems

Difficulty in engag-
ing or changing
gear

CLUTCH & TRANSMISSION

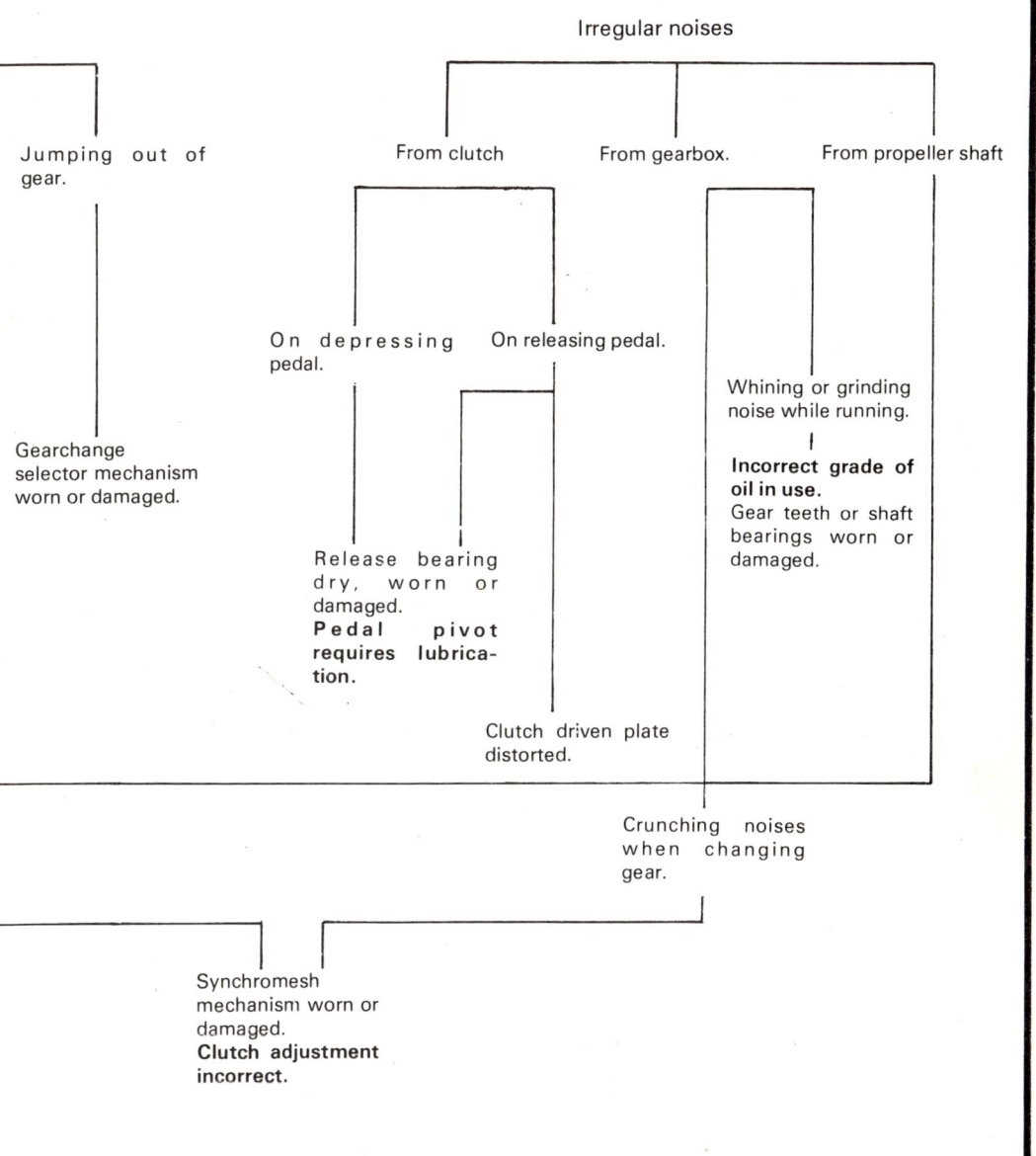

Irregular noises

Jumping out of gear.

From clutch

From gearbox.

From propeller shaft

On depressing pedal.

On releasing pedal.

Gearchange selector mechanism worn or damaged.

Whining or grinding noise while running.

Incorrect grade of oil in use.
Gear teeth or shaft bearings worn or damaged.

Release bearing dry, worn or damaged.
Pedal pivot requires lubrication.

Clutch driven plate distorted.

Crunching noises when changing gear.

Synchromesh mechanism worn or damaged.
Clutch adjustment incorrect.

TROUBLESHOOTER 4:

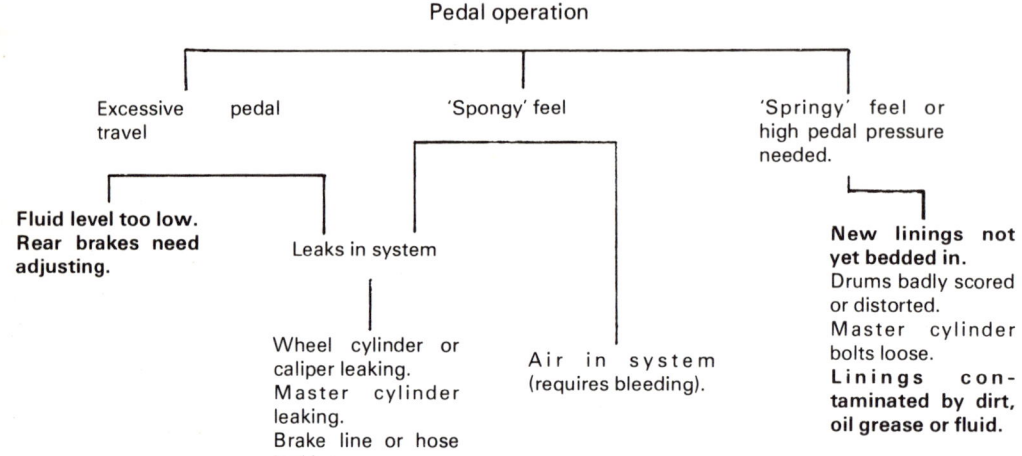

Pedal operation

Excessive pedal travel

'Spongy' feel

'Springy' feel or high pedal pressure needed.

Fluid level too low. Rear brakes need adjusting.

Leaks in system

Wheel cylinder or caliper leaking. Master cylinder leaking. Brake line or hose leaking.

Air in system (requires bleeding).

New linings not yet bedded in. Drums badly scored or distorted. Master cylinder bolts loose. **Linings contaminated by dirt, oil grease or fluid.**

TROUBLESHOOTER 5:

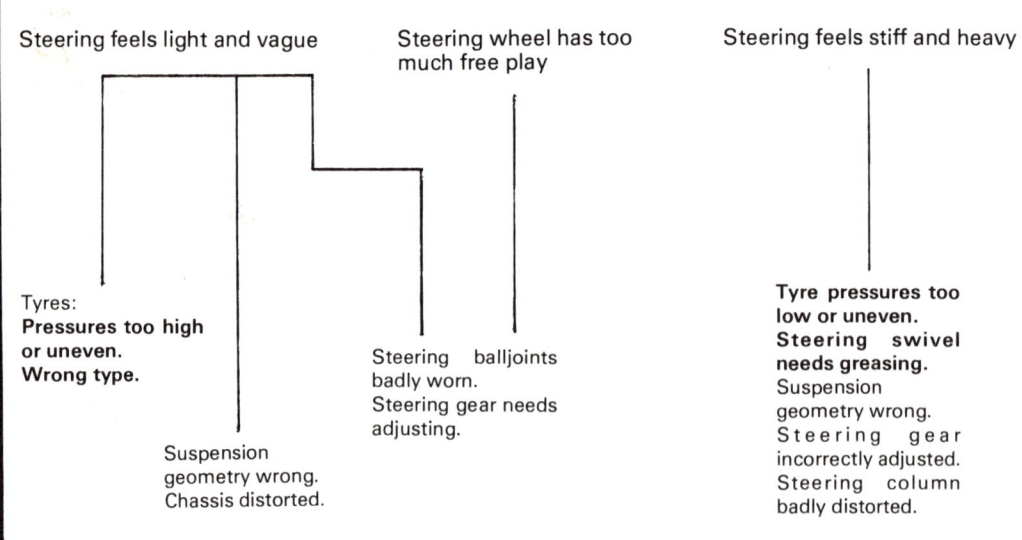

Steering feels light and vague

Steering wheel has too much free play

Steering feels stiff and heavy

Tyres: **Pressures too high or uneven. Wrong type.**

Suspension geometry wrong. Chassis distorted.

Steering balljoints badly worn. Steering gear needs adjusting.

Tyre pressures too low or uneven. Steering swivel needs greasing. Suspension geometry wrong. Steering gear incorrectly adjusted. Steering column badly distorted.

BRAKES

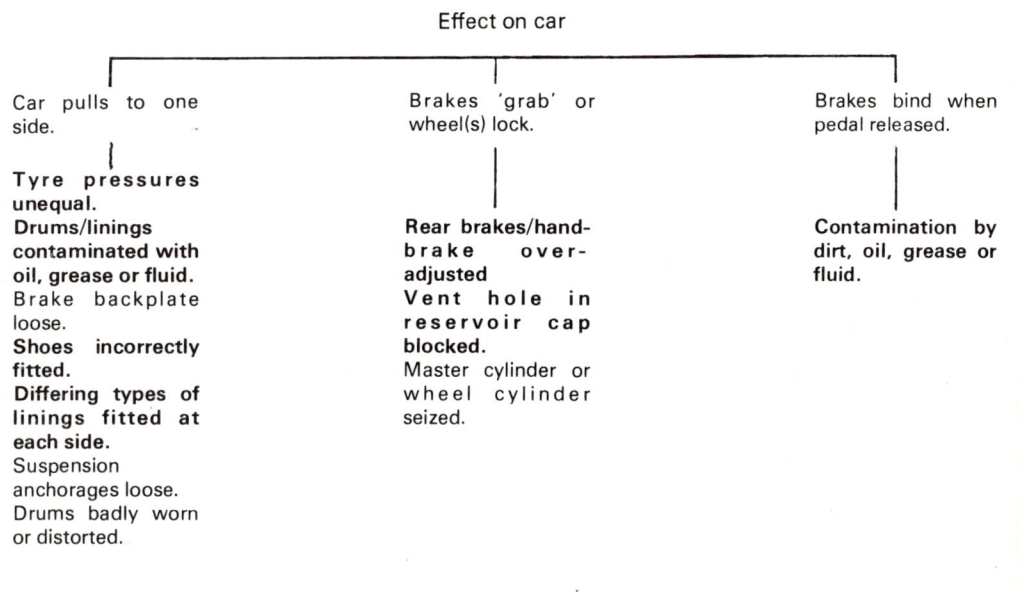

Effect on car

Car pulls to one side.

Tyre pressures unequal.
Drums/linings contaminated with oil, grease or fluid.
Brake backplate loose.
Shoes incorrectly fitted.
Differing types of linings fitted at each side.
Suspension anchorages loose.
Drums badly worn or distorted.

Brakes 'grab' or wheel(s) lock.

Rear brakes/hand-brake over-adjusted
Vent hole in reservoir cap blocked.
Master cylinder or wheel cylinder seized.

Brakes bind when pedal released.

Contamination by dirt, oil, grease or fluid.

STEERING/SUSPENSION

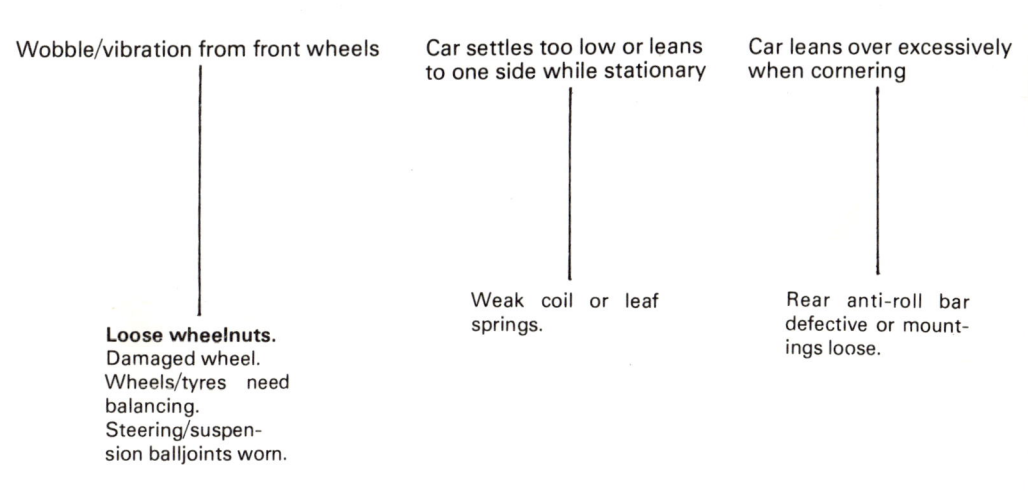

Wobble/vibration from front wheels

Car settles too low or leans to one side while stationary

Car leans over excessively when cornering

Loose wheelnuts.
Damaged wheel.
Wheels/tyres need balancing.
Steering/suspension balljoints worn.

Weak coil or leaf springs.

Rear anti-roll bar defective or mountings loose.

TROUBLESHOOTER 6:

NOTE: This chart assumes that the battery installed in your car is in good condition and of the correct specification, and that the terminal connections are clean and tight. A car used frequently for stop-start motoring or for short journeys (particularly during the winter when lights, heater blower etc are likely to be in use) may need its battery recharged at intervals to keep it serviceable. If an electrical problem occurs, don't immediately suspect the starter or any other component without first checking that the battery's capable of supplying its demands!

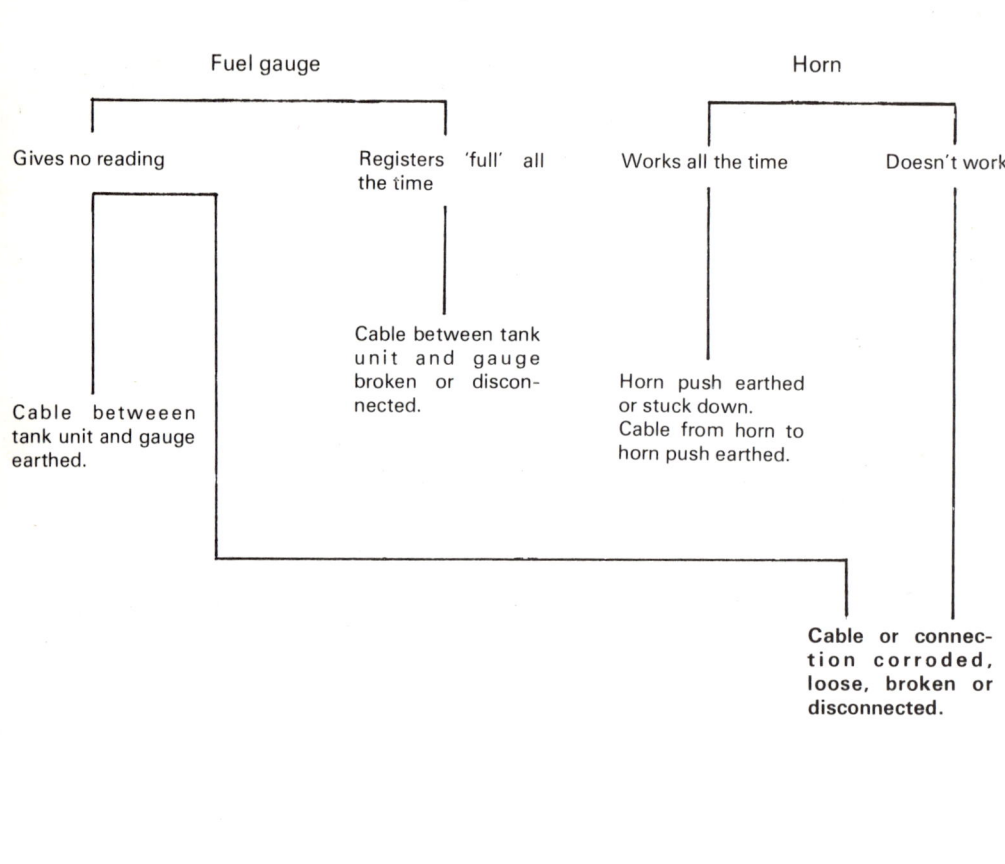

Fuel gauge

Horn

Gives no reading

Registers 'full' all the time

Works all the time

Doesn't work

Cable between tank unit and gauge broken or discon-nected.

Horn push earthed or stuck down.
Cable from horn to horn push earthed.

Cable betweeen tank unit and gauge earthed.

Cable or connec-tion corroded, loose, broken or disconnected.

ELECTRICS

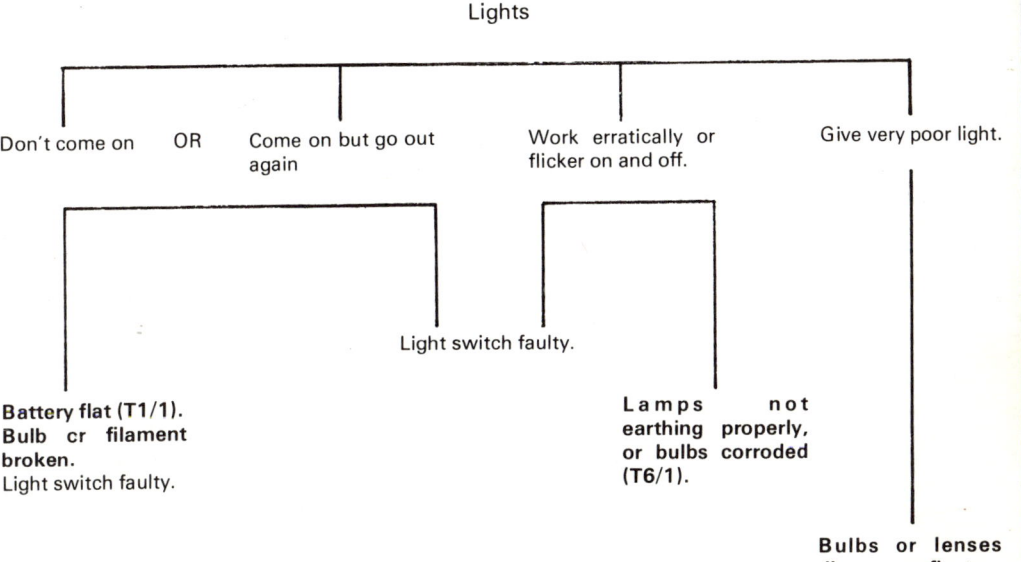

Lights

Don't come on   OR   Come on but go out   Work erratically or   Give very poor light.
                                  again   flicker on and off.

Light switch faulty.

Battery flat (T1/1).
Bulb cr filament
broken.
Light switch faulty.

Lamps   not
earthing properly,
or bulbs corroded
(T6/1).

Bulbs or lenses
dirty or reflectors
dirty or corrroded.
Wrong   bulbs
installed.

Because of the glass fibre bodies employed on these Reliant models, the separate earthing leads fitted to electrical components, including lights, are particularly important. A fault occurring in any other electrical equipment or accessory not specifically referred to above can usually be traced to one of three main causes, i.e: blown fuse; loose or broken connection to power supply or earth; or internal fault in the component concerned.

CROSS REFERENCE TABLE

TROUBLESHOOTER
REFERENCE

ADDITIONAL
INFORMATION

TROUBLESHOOTER
REFERENCE

ADDITIONAL
INFORMATION

T1/1 Either charge the battery from a battery charger, or use jump leads to start the car from another battery; make sure that the lead polarities are correct in both cases or you may do permanent damage, particularly if your car has an alternator.

T1/2 If lead's loose, disconnect the battery earth lead then tighten the connection on the starter motor. Make sure that the bolt doesn't turn while you're tightening the nut. Reconnect the battery earth lead.

T1/3 You can use a spanner on the square-ended shaft on the end of the starter motor. By turning it you'll normally be able to free it from the flywheel ring gear.

T1/4 Make sure that all the connections are tight, then wipe the leads clean and dry with a lint-free cloth. Use an ignition system waterproofer (e.g. WD40 or Damp-Start) to prevent problems in the future.

T1/5 An ignition coil is a simple item to fit, but make a note of the connections before removing them, and ensure that the replacement coil's the correct type. Renewal of the condenser is covered in the 6000-mile Service Schedule (Item 5).

T1/6 To check the operation of the pump, detach the fuel outlet pipe (that's the one that goes to the carburettor) and operate it manually with the small lever on the side if there is one. If there's no lever, turn the engine over on the starter a few times. There should be a steady stream of petrol if the pump's

working properly. Cleaning the fuel filter is covered in the 12 000-mile Service Schedule (Item 6).

T1/7 It's easy enough to tighten the attachment bolts if you've got a box or socket spanner of the right size; if you haven't, it's not really a D-I-Y job.

T2/1 For temporary repair a leaking hose can normally be bound up with adhesive tape or, better still, with a hose bandage available for this purpose. Wait till the system's cooled down, then top it up. If it happens a second time, get it looked at straight away or you could ruin your engine (if it hasn't happened already).

T2/2 Driving carefully will probably get you home. An airline on the radiator core will clean out the dirt that's accumulated; if it's blocked internally, use a proprietary flushing compound.

T2/3 You may be able to repair the hose temporarily (see T2/1) but it'll almost certainly mean a new one.

T2/4 Drive more slowly — but without labouring the engine.

T6/1 Remove the lamp lenses and bulbs (see *In an Emergency*) and check for signs of rust. Where there's rust, scrape it off and apply a little petroleum jelly (Vaseline). Ensure that the cables earthing the lamp body are making good connections.

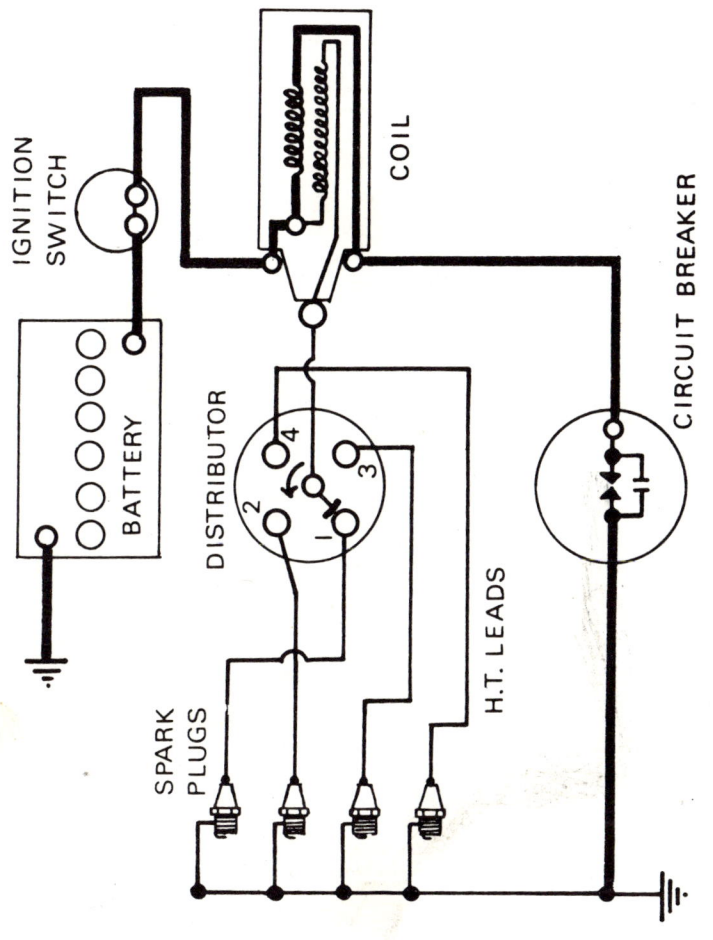

IGNITION SWITCH

BATTERY

COIL

DISTRIBUTOR

CIRCUIT BREAKER

H.T. LEADS

SPARK PLUGS

Diagram of the ignition circuits. The LT is indicated by the heavier lines

CONVERSION

Distance

Inches (in)	X 25.400	=	Millimetres (mm)
Feet (ft)	X 0.305	=	Metres (m)
Miles	X 1.609	=	Kilometres (km)
Millimetres (mm)	X 0.039	=	Inches (in)
Metres (m)	X 3.281	=	Feet (ft)
Kilometres (km)	X 0.621	=	Miles

Capacity

Inches, cubic (cu in/in^3)	X 16.387	=	Centimetres, cubic (cc/cm^3)
Fluid ounce, imperial (fl oz)	X 35.51	=	Centimetres, cubic (cc/cm^3)
Fluid ounce, US (fl oz)	X 29.57	=	Centimetres, cubic (cc/cm^3)
Pints, imperial (imp pt)	X 0.568	=	Litres (L)
Quarts, imperial (imp qt)	X 1.1365	=	Litres (L)
Quarts, imperial (imp qt)	X 1.201	=	Quart, US (US qt)
Quarts, US (US qt)	X 0.9463	=	Litres (L)
Quarts, US (US qt)	X 0.8326	=	Quarts, imperial (imp qt)
Gallons, imperial (imp gal)	X 4.546	=	Litres (L)
Gallons, imperial (imp gal)	X 1.201	=	Gallons, US (US gal)
Gallons, US (US gal)	X 3.7853	=	Litres (L)
Gallons, US (US gal)	X 0.8326	=	Gallons, imperial (imp gal)
Centimetres, cubic (cc/cm^3)	X 0.061	=	Inches, cubic (cu in/in^3)
Centimetres, cubic (cc/cm^3)	X 0.02816	=	Fluid ounces, imperial (fl oz)
Centimeters, cubic (cc/cm^3)	X 0.03381	=	Fluid ounces, US (fl oz)
Litres (L)	X 28.16	=	Fluid ounces, imperial (fl oz)
Litres (L)	X 33.81	=	Fluid ounces, US (fl oz)
Litres (L)	X 1.760	=	Pints, imperial (imp pt)
Litres (L)	X 0.8799	=	Quarts, imperial (imp qt)
Litres (L)	X 1.0567	=	Quarts, US (US qt)
Litres (L)	X 0.220	=	Gallons, imperial (imp gal)
Litres (L)	X 0.264	=	Gallons, US (US gal)

Area

Inches, square (in^2/sq in)	X 645.160	=	Millimetres, square (mm^2/sq mm)
Feet, square (ft^2/sq ft)	X 0.093	=	Metres, square (m^2/sq m)
Millimetres, square (mm^2/sq mm)	X 0.002	=	Inches, square (in^2/sq in)
Metres, square (m^2/sq m)	X 10.764	=	Feet square (ft^2/sq ft)

Weight

Ounces (oz)	X 28.350	=	Grammes (g)
Pounds (lbs)	X 0.454	=	Kilogrammes (kg)
Grammes (g)	X 0.035	=	Ounces (oz)
Kilogrammes (kg)	X 2.205	=	Pounds (lbs)
Kilogrammes (kg)	X 35.274	=	Ounces (oz)

FACTORS

Pressure

Pounds/sq in (psi/lb/sq in/ lb/in²)	X 0.070	= Kilogrammes/sq cm (kg/sq cm)
Pounds/sq in (psi/lb/sq in/ lb/in²)	X 0.068	= Atmospheres (atm)
Kilogrammes sq cm (kg/sq cm)	X 14.223	= Pounds/sq in (psi/lb/sq in/ lb/in²)
Atmospheres (atm)	X 14.696	= Pounds/sq in (psi/lb/sq in/ lb/in²)

Torque

Pound - inches (lbf in)	X 0.0115	= Kilogramme - metres (kgf m)
Pound - inches (lbf in)	X 0.0833	= Pound - feet (lbf ft)
Pound - feet (lbf ft)	X 12	= Pound - inches (lbf in)
Pound - feet (lbf ft)	X 0.138	= Kilogramme - metres (kgf m)
Pound - feet (lbf ft)	X 1.356	= Newton - metres (Nm)
Kilogramme - metres (kgf m)	X 86.796	= Pound - inches (lbf in)
Kilogramme - metres (kgf m)	X 7.233	= Pound - feet (lbf ft)
Newton - metres (Nm)	X 0.738	= Pound - feet (lbf ft)
Newton - metres (Nm)	X 0.102	= Kilogramme - metres (kgf m)

Speed

Miles - hour (mph)	X 1.609	= Kilometres - hour (kph)
Feet - second	X 0.305	= Metres - second (m/s)
Kilometres - hour (kph)	X 0.621	= Miles - hour (mph)
Metres - second (m/s)	X 3.281	= Feet - second
Metres - second (m/s)	X 3.600	= Kilometres - hour (kph)

Consumption

Miles - gallon, imperial (mpg)	X 0.354	= Kilometres - litre (km/l)
Kilometres - litre (km/l)	X 2.825	= Miles - gallon, imperial (mpg)

Temperature

Centigrade (°C) to Fahrenheit (°F)

$$\frac{9}{5}\ °C + 32 = °F$$

Fahrenheit (°F) to Centigrade (°C)

$$\frac{5}{9}\ (°F - 32) = °C$$

Index

Printed by
Haynes Publishing Group
Sparkford Yeovil Somerset
England